EPISCOPALIANS AND ROMAN CATHOLICS:

Can They Ever Get Together?

EPISCOPALIANS AND ROMAN CATHOLICS:

Can They Ever Get Together?

Edited by HERBERT J. RYAN, S.J.,

and J. ROBERT WRIGHT

DIMENSION BOOKS
DENVILLE, NEW JERSEY

Published by Dimension Books Inc.

Denville, New Jersey

FIRST EDITION SEPTEMBER 1972

Dedicated to

POPE PAUL VI

and

ARTHUR MICHAEL RAMSEY,
Archbishop of Canterbury

CONTENTS

Foreword

This volume is designed to share with interested clergy and laity the results of informal and unofficial bilateral conversations between fourteen speakers and thirty-four representative participants of the Roman Catholic and Episcopal Churches in the United States which were held at Graymoor on May 8-12, 1972. The concern of the conversations was to provide for ecumenical study groups an inexpensive yet professional presentation of the contemporary situation facing both churches which would be informative and projective.

The conversations, which were co-sponsored by the Graymoor Ecumenical Institute and the Episcopal Church Foundation, were in large measure a response to the visit of Dr. Michael Ramsey, the Archbishop of Canterbury, to Graymoor on January 26, 1972, to receive the Unity Award presented in memory of Father Paul James Francis, founder of the Society of the Atonement and pioneer apostle of Christian unity in the United States.

It is hoped that this volume will contribute some tangible form to the process of growing together which members of both traditions ardently seek and that the questions and responses which this volume may elicit will be useful in planning further conversations of this kind in the future. May our mutual efforts move us onwards to the realization of Christ's prayer "that all may be one."

RALPH THOMAS, S.A.

Graymoor Ecumenical Institute

EPISCOPALIANS AND ROMAN CATHOLICS:

Can They Ever Get Together?

I

CONTOURS FOR TOMORROW

The New Dynamics of Anglican - Roman Catholic Dialogue

by
HERBERT J. RYAN, S.J.

SUMMARY

This paper summarizes the official national and international Anglican-Roman Catholic dialogues by answering three questions: (1) What have they accomplished? (2) What is their present agenda? (3) What are their future prospects? Future prospects for the "organic union" of the Episcopal Church and the Roman Catholic Church are seen to hinge on the spiritual renewal of both Churches and their mutual rededication to evangelism and service to the cause of social justice. But renewal and rededication will not insure the "organic union" of the two Churches unless Episcopalian and Roman Catholic laity judge it to be supportive of their spiritual needs and of the service they feel as Christians they owe their neighbors in the local community.

When Roman Catholics and Episcopalians look together to the future it would be natural for them to ask if there had been a group of their fellows who had been engaged in the task of trying to see whether the present

7

course of their Churches would lead to a common future for both. Such groups do exist on both the national and international levels. Two official dialogue groups are attempting to analyze the present situation and aid in the future convergence of the Roman Catholic and the Episcopal Churches. In order to see what contours for tomorrow these groups believe to be emerging perhaps our first task should be to investigate what ARC on the national level and ARCIC on the international have been doing. Such an approach to the problem of what the future may hold in store would give a sense of reality to projections concerning the decade to come and forestall objections about writing of this type being only an exercise in imagination or an essay in futurology. As a first step in tracing the contours for tomorrow three questions could be asked of the national (ARC) and international (ARCIC) dialogue groups. (1) What have they accomplished? (2) What is their present agenda? (3) What are their future prospects? The first part of this essay will be a Roman Catholic attempt to answer these questions.

ARC, or the Joint Commission on Anglican-Roman Catholic Relations, is jointly sponsored by the Commission on Ecumenical Relations of the Episcopal Church and the Roman Catholic Bishops' Committee for Ecumenical and Interreligious Affairs. This committee has met eleven times since June of 1965. During the course of their seventh meeting in December 1969, the members of ARC drew up a report to their sponsoring bodies.[1] This report was "gratefully and enthusiastically" accepted by the Roman Catholic Bishops' Committee on Ecumenical and Interreligious Affairs on March 18, 1970[2] and the 63rd General Convention of the Episcopal Church which met at Houston in October of 1970 voted

three resolutions in support of the ARC VII report.[3]
What ARC has accomplished might properly be seen in
the light of the ARC VII report. In the report the purpose of this bilateral consultation is clearly stated.
". . . We see the goal as to realize full communion of the
Roman Catholic Church with the Episcopal Church and
the other Churches of the Anglican Communion."[4] Yet
this goal was not considered to be incompatible with the
wide range of ecumenical commitments that both our
Churches had undertaken. "At the same time, we hasten
to add that we cannot conceive our efforts in this bilateral consultation as divorced from the other significant
efforts which in our times we are privileged to witness
being made to achieve the goal of further reconciliation
and full ecclesial unity among all Christians. We would
never wish our own specific efforts and our own specific
goal to be regarded as prejudicial to the many different
efforts that are being made by our Churches toward this
end. Specifically, we wish to mention in this regard the
Consultation on Church Union, in which the Episcopal
Church is engaged, and the other bilateral consultations
in which both our Churches are honored to participate.
All of these endeavors have been a source of gratification
to the members of ARC and we, in turn, hope that our
endeavor may be seen as a source of encouragement
to them."[5]

In the report of ARC VII there were three sections
which mapped out the work which the members of ARC
saw that they should undertake. The first task was to
study and appreciate other contemporary Church union
dialogues. The second task was the theological development of a model for organic union. This theological
model (not a sociologically based scheme for church gov-

ernment) would have to provide us with a way to show our unity in faith, celebrate our sacramental life together and equip our communicants for a multifaceted witness in carrying out Christ's mission to the world. Yet this model would have to respect both the Anglican and Roman tradition and experience. Furthermore, this model for union would have to be such as to keep both Churches open to other Churches so that they as Churches could join us in a partnership of mutual support for evangelization, spiritual renewal of ourselves and community action. The third task was diffusion of the ARC project throughout the dioceses and parishes of the Episcopal and Roman Catholic Churches, that is, eliciting grass roots support, encouraging local initiative and communicating to others the ways that some communities had succeeded in bringing Episcopalians and Roman Catholics to see that their common Christian faith holds the promise of a mutual Christian witness for tomorrow's world.

The last four meetings of ARC have been devoted to the theological work that ARC pledged it would attempt. ARC XI has published "Doctrinal Agreement and Christian Unity: Methodological Considerations," a document which attempts to lay the groundwork for our mutual understanding of the one Christian faith we profess, though expressed in different ways.[6] On the basis of their methodology ARC XII will begin to consider the Roman and Episcopal Churches at two *typoi* within the one communion of the Church.[7] ARC's goal in doing this is to find the principles by which the Roman Catholic and the Episcopal Churches can recognize one another as Churches and, hopefully, have other Churches also accept these principles and contribute their experience and understanding of the Gospel and their form of Church life and mission to the visible communion of love which is the Church of Christ.

The third task, that of diffusion of the ARC project, has been varied. A retreat for Episcopal and Roman bishops,[8] clergy conferences for Episcopalians and Romans in Cleveland, New York, Louisville, Richmond and Worcester,[9] regional conferences of ecumenical officers especially in the New England area,[10] the setting up of diocesan ARC dialogue groups,[11] the publication of ARC-DOC[12] and other dialogue materials and in two dioceses the spiritual covenanting of parishes[13] have been attempts to test the ARC project in the day to day life of the Church. ARC members have expended themselves in this effort of diffusion but despite these personal endeavors it would be unfair to report that the task of diffusion has met with a wide measure of success. In this sphere or area diffusion has not been widespread enough, especially in Roman Catholic circles, to say that ARC has been successful in this task it set itself two and a half years ago.

ARC defined its goal as "full communion of the Roman Catholic Church with the Episcopal Church and the other Churches of the Anglican Communion." What has ARC achieved for the other Churches of the Anglican Communion and for the Roman Catholic Church outside of the United States? ARC has been the model which other nations or regions have imitated in the growing pattern of bilateral dialogues between the Roman Catholic Church and the Churches of the Anglican Communion. This conscious imitation is evident in South Africa, England, Canada and the Joint Working Group in Belgium, France and Holland. Though conscious imitation by others of the method and program of ARC is a measure of its achievement, the spreading of the ARC project would most likely not have occurred if ARC had not had the continuing influence on the International Commission which it has exercised from 1967 until the present time. When the Secretariat for Promoting Christian Unity sought a Roman Catholic chairman for the Anglican-Roman Catholic Joint Preparatory Commission the Roman Catholic bishop who was most experienced in this regard was the co-chairman of ARC, Bishop Charles Helmsing of Kansas City - St. Joseph. Under the guidance of Bishop Helmsing and with the aid of Fr. George Tavard, a member of ARC, the "Malta Report" (as the Preparatory Commission's final report is called) set the agenda for ARCIC, as the Anglican-Roman Catholic International Commission is now named. The agenda of ARCIC — to reach consensus on doctrine concerning Eucharist, Ministry and Authority — represents the experience of ARC until 1968. In a sense, ARCIC exists because ARC proved it could exist and the three members of ARC who are on the International Commission have of necessity influenced its deliberations in the light of their own experience in the ARC dialogue.

What has ARCIC achieved? From the point of view of the Secretariat for Promoting Christian Unity ARCIC is one of four dialogues which the Roman See is conducting with world confessional families: Anglicans, Methodists, Presbyterians or Reformed, and Lutherans. It is the most advanced of these dialogues and it has a clear agenda: to oversee the relations between the two Communions, Roman and Anglican, and to offer by way of consensus statements after responsible research a way through the doctrinal difficulties that many feel stand as a barrier to organic union between the Roman and Anglican Communions. ARCIC has already published its initial statements on Eucharist, Ministry and Church.[14] The doctrinal consensus on the Eucharist was released in late December 1971 to be studied by the Churches and hopefully win acceptance after it has been analyzed. At least the document may act as a catalyst for many Romans and Episcopalians to see that loyalty to our traditions and doctrines does not imply denial of the substance of the faith but rather underscores how very great indeed is the measure of our agreement once we understand what the other is trying to say.[15]

What is the present agenda of ARC and ARCIC? ARC is at work on a model of union for the Episcopal Church and the Roman Catholic Church — a model that will safeguard the identity and traditions of both Churches and commend itself to other Churches to join in our common mission of commitment to Christ and his world. ARCIC is now working on the consensus statement on ministry, a part of which must concern itself with the ordained ministry and for Roman Catholics, the emotion-charged question which one may incorrectly refer to as the validity of Anglican orders, or put more correctly, though not comprehensively, the acceptance of the Episcopal Church as a sister Church in the one Communion of Christ.

What are the future prospects for ARC and ARCIC? The most difficult question that both the national and the international dialogue groups face is the defining of the mission of the Church in the contemporary world. The Roman Church grappled with this question at the Second Vatican Council. The result is the Pastoral Constitution *Gaudium et Spes*. The Anglican Communion wrestled with this question at the Tenth Lambeth Conference in 1968. The documents of this Conference bear a striking resemblance to those of the Second Vatican Council and many of the themes of *Gaudium et Spes* were treated in a similar fashion in the section reports which the Tenth Lambeth Conference issued. The documents of Vatican II and Lambeth '68 certainly show the convergence of Roman Catholic and Anglican theology.[16] Yet this theology underscores more than a growing consciousness of a similarity in religious sensitivity, pastoral approach and theological method. Most significantly, perhaps, both Vatican II and Lambeth '68 point up the difficulty of explaining in concrete, pastorally realizable terms on the diocesan and parish level the difference that the existence of a Christian community makes to the local community of which it is a part. Both Vatican II and Lambeth '68 proclaim a breathtaking vision of the Church. In spelling out this vision both assemblies utilized the resources of modern Biblical studies and the insights of the social sciences. Yet despite the freshness and beauty of this vision of the Church the documents of Vatican II or Lambeth '68 contain little that bears directly on the mission of the local Church or the program of an individual diocese or parish. The future prospects of ARC and ARCIC are tied directly to programs and priorities of regional Churches, dioceses and parishes. ARC and ARCIC must show that the organic union of the Roman Catholic Church and the Churches of the Anglican Communion will make a significant contribution to the work on the national, diocesan and parish level which the Roman Catholic Church in the United States and the Episcopal Church, the diocese of

Worcester and the Diocese of Western Massachusetts, St. Anthony of Padua's and St. Andrew-in-the-Field's are attempting to do for Christ and his world.

It is good theology to emphasize that the unity which Christ wills for his Church is a unity which He will give his Church. But it is also good theology not to overstress one principle. One may lay so much stress on the divinity of Christ that his humanity is underplayed. So too one may so stress the eschatalogical element of the unity of the Church, the divine character of the elements of the Church universal, the divine initiative in creating and sustaining the mystery which is the Church that the result would be an ecclesiological docetism. ARC and ARCIC would have no future in an ecclesiology of a docetist stamp. These dialogue groups are working towards future union of quite visible congregations of very real people. They must show what difference to the lives of Nick and Maria Lombardi and Fred and Edith Appleton the union of the Roman Catholic and Episcopal Churches will make. More fundamentally still, they must show the Lombardis and the Appletons what difference their being members of St. Anthony's or communicants of St. Andrew's makes in the community in which they live. For if their belonging to Christian parishes within their local community has no meaning for or impact on the community at large, what perceptible difference would their parishes coming into sacramental sharing or a special relationship as sister congregations have? Nick and Maria, Fred and Edith are not immediately or directly helped by the documents of Vatican II or Lambeth '68 to see that the union of the Roman Catholic Church and the Episcopal Church will help them, St. Anthony's or St. Andrew's. If ARC and

ARCIC are to advance the unity of Christ's Church they must show the millions of people like the Lombardis and the Appletons what advantage to the work of Christ in their lives the union of the two Churches would bring.

Still as important as is the sense of the local significance of the organic union of the Roman Catholic Church and the Episcopal Church, ARC and ARCIC must also provide the local congregations and individual dioceses with a feeling for the truly catholic mission of the Church universal. The delicate interplay of local relevance and world-wide significance provides ARC and ARCIC with a thrust for renewal of the whole Church. The parish, the diocese, the national Church, if ARC and ARCIC are taken as seriously as they are meant to be, would be called to a period of scrutiny and prayerful reflection to examine themselves and their mission or outreach in light of proposals for organic union. Thus the first outlines that can be discerned in contours for tomorrow would deal with the spiritual renewal of the Church.

In the day to day life of the Church one can foresee in the immediate future an increase in the frequency and intensity of Roman Catholics and Episcopalians praying together. There will be more retreats for bishops and clergy, more conferences for spiritual renewal, more prayer groups whose members will come from both an Episcopalian and Roman Catholic parish. One may also foresee an increased desire on the part of faithful Roman Catholics and Episcopalians to share the Eucharist together.

Before sacramental sharing is possible the Roman Catholic Church will have to have accepted the ordained ministry of the Episcopal Church as on a par with its own. For this to happen the Roman Catholic Church would have to clarify its own understanding of the ordained ministry in the light of its developing ecclesiology. "The theology of the ministry forms part of the theology of the Church and must be considered as such."[17] Even if this extremely difficult theological work could be completed swiftly the process of growing together in genuine love and mutual respect will require time. Another outline of the contours for tomorrow will be the steadily increasing contacts of the bishops and clergy of the Roman Catholic and Episcopal Churches. To see one another as sharing in the same priestly ministry of Christ the clergy of the two Churches must know, respect and love one another as brother priests in Christ. In the emerging pattern of relations of the two Churches it would not be unlikely that the bishops of the two Churches on a diocesan and regional level would begin to enter into a relationship of mutual counseling and support. The pastoral experience of retired Episcopal bishops would be a valuable resource for younger Roman Catholic bishops to rely upon. It would not be surprising to see a formal relationship across denominational lines developing between the younger and the more experienced bishops to the benefit of both Churches. Under the leadership of the hierarchy a similar pattern may well emerge among the pastors and rectors of parishes and the parochial clergy in general.

As trust of one another grows among the clerical leaders of the two Churches, greater cooperation in the training of candidates for Orders will come as a matter of course. But perhaps the most significant development in education will be the sharing of personnel and programs

17

for the Christian instruction of youth and continuing adult education. One can forecast an ecumenical use of the Catholic Parochial School System which in the next decade will most probably be regarded as a resource for urban Christian mission for the entire Christian community. The schools may well become centers for a panoply of Christian programs in the inner city and not exclusively educational institutions maintained solely by Roman Catholic parishes and dioceses. What had once been viewed by some Christians as a sign of denominational divisiveness may well become the focus and base of an intense ecumenical effort in the Christian service of social justice.

If present experience of the spiritual covenanting of parishes is a guide to future projection, this form of local parish cooperation will spread throughout the country. At present the cooperation is limited to mutual prayer by the two parishes in the covenant relationship, mutual planning on the part of the Roman Catholic pastor and the Episcopal rector for parish visitation, charitable concerns and projects for social welfare, and exchange of observers at parish council and vestry meetings. One can anticipate that such a relationship will grow to the extent of both the parish council and the vestry jointly sponsoring long-term programs for social justice in the local community. The pattern of action that will develop most probably will be open to other Churches in the area, especially if the cost and long-term commitment of the project will require a wide community base and financial resources exceeding those available to only two parishes. The same pattern may well develop between Roman Catholic and Episcopal dioceses.

On the parochial level but with diocesan support one

may well see before 1980 ecumenical parishes and an ecumenical team ministry of Roman Catholics and Episcopalians. This new form of parish ministry may take its rise in the inner city but it would seem that newer suburban sections might request of the Roman and Episcopal diocesan bishops this form of Church life not only as a witness to the two Churches' commitment to organic union but as an act of responsible stewardship in not building two separate parochial plants. The trend towards the non-duplication of facilities may extend itself to the wider Christian community and what one could find by 1980 is that in newly built residential areas one constructs a Christian Center rather than a cluster of denominational parish facilities.

Such are but a few of the contours for tomorrow. Yet the most important of these contours has yet to be mentioned. To speak truthfully about it one must confess that at present it exists only in the most inchoate form. Roman Catholics and Episcopalians will have to develop together a spirituality, a form of Christian motivation for maturity in Christ in order for their two Churches mutually to support one another in their common carrying out of Christ's mission in the world. The problems of two communities, two religious families, two Christian traditions in the communion of the one Church of Christ consciously striving to appreciate the spirituality and pastoral style of the other are almost too numerous to list. The role of authority in the spiritual tradition of each Church, the way in which the two Churches school Christian conscience, their traditional methods for discerning the movement of the Holy Spirit in the individual Christian's life show more differences than similarities. Yet it is almost a foregone conclusion that if pastoral patience with one another and genuine interior sharing concerning the Christian experience proves impossible to sustain, then the two Churches, Roman and Episcopalian, will not be able to grow into organic union. Common programs, jointly owned buildings, even common prayer together will fall apart at the seams unless the deeper realities of the Christian life which Romans and Episcopalians experience can be spoken of in the intimacy of Christian community.

Such are some of the contours for tomorrow which at least one Roman Catholic sees as his Church and the Episcopal Church move towards organic union as sister Churches in the one communion of the Church of Christ.

Where We Have Been: Where We Are Going

by

STEPHEN F. BAYNE, JR.

SUMMARY

Three guidelines to successful ecumenical development are briefly discussed — that "nothing is real which is not local," that all such development is a process of discovery or learning, and that serious ecumenical work is not born out of a dilletantish frivolity but rather out of intense seriousness and even pain. Four broad areas are then proposed as areas where joint Anglican-Roman Catholic activity would seem especially important and fruitful, from an Episcopalian point of view. They are, first, a consideration of mission, especially in terms of empowerment or liberation. Second, the continuing exploration of confessional theology (such as the joint Eucharistic statement) is of special significance to Episcopalians. Third, attention needs to be paid to the question of authority, specifically in ministry and in moral theology. Finally, both churches need a renewed and positive commitment to prayer, together. The discussion closes with a second look at the three guidelines and particularly at the urgent importance of keeping our objectives and our motivation clear and affirmative.

It is the task of ARC and ARCIC to be official stewards of the mutual ecumenical imaginings and projections of the Anglican and Roman Catholic Churches. I mean by this that it lies in their hands to determine the direction of our joint ecumenical work, to test our models and our words, to guide our energies, to frame our goals and set our course as we go along. Without that responsible stewardship, the spasmodic reflections of ecumenically-minded people like myself would be vaporous and jerky and of little consequence. But given the kind of steady leadership ARC provides, there is a place for amateurs, for the unofficial imaginers.

Indeed there may be a need for them if the Anglican-Roman dialogue is not to suffer the malady of other ecumenical conversations—of becoming unintentionally the preserve of a select few who by their very easiness and their accomplishments tend to discourage what is referred to as "grass-roots" ecumenism. I suspect that this agricultural image has somewhat supercilious overtones and perhaps is sometimes meant to do so. In fact, however, it refers to one of the essential characteristics of true ecumenical development — that "nothing is real which is not local". Fr. Ryan in his paper deals very fully with this and the danger of "ecclesiastical docetism", and I am content simply to state my own conviction as to the necessity of both the official and the utterly unofficial conversation going on continuously. For my own part I am quite happy to peer up at the Olympians on the "top-level" from my nest among the ants, and say what I want to say.

It is a commonplace to say that any projection of the contours of tomorrow can only be a triangulation from where we are now. The image a man has of the common future of our two churches is likely to be not much more than a reflection of what he cares most about now. This is not to apologize for one's thoughts. It is to underline a second characteristic of true ecumenical development, that it is an unceasing process of learning, sometimes painful, sometimes explosively illuminating, always unexpected and always a gift of the Spirit.

For Anglicans, this was foreshadowed in the 1920 Appeal to All Christian People, one of the climactic documents of Anglican ecumenical history. "The vision which rises before us is that of a Church, genuinely Catholic, loyal to all Truth, and gathering into its fellowship all 'who profess and call themselves Christians', within whose visible unity all the treasures of faith and order, bequeathed as a heritage by the past to the present, shall be possessed in common, and made serviceable to the whole Body of Christ. Within this unity Christian Communions now separated from one another would retain much that has long been distinctive in their methods of worship and service. It is through a rich diversity of life and devotion that the unity of the whole fellowship will be fulfilled. *This means an adventure of goodwill and still more of faith, for nothing less is required than a new discovery of the creative resources of God*" (italics mine).

This vision and the adventure of faith enshrined in the Appeal a half-century ago were quick to catch the imagination of many millions of people. But their translation from rhetoric into daily life and work turned out to be far more costly and far more portentous than anyone could have guessed. Many people are unsettled by ecumenical adventure, even frightened by it; and nowhere is this more evident than in our own American scene where large numbers of people are what they are ecclesiastically after having been something else which they didn't like being. Alternatively, they are what they are because being that plays a decisive role in giving them their identity. In either case they peer out at the "rich diversity of life and devotion" outside their windows with distaste and suspicion, and keep the doors locked.

To those who persevere in the adventure, life-giving discoveries are possible — at least they are possible if the adventure be genuinely one of faith and not one born out of boredom or spiritual frivolity. This may even be a third characteristic of true ecumenical development, that it is not fostered by thrill-seeking and it does not proceed without anguish.

At any rate I take my three rubrics as guides to my own thoughts. True ecumenical development must be genuinely local as well as general, it must be the result of new learnings, and it must be born out of an intense seriousness and even pain. What I say of tomorrow's contours is disciplined by those precepts.

There are four general areas where, from the point of view of the Episcopal Church, we have the most to hope for from deeper unity, and it is in these areas that the most significant developments will probably lie. The first is what is generally referred to as Mission. In a recent statement adopted by our Executive Council it is stated that "Empowerment is the predominant objective in the ministry and mission of our church at home and abroad in our day". The statement characterizes Empowerment as "a liberating process for oppressed and oppressor, for powerful and powerless, whereby God's Spirit breaks the walls of separation that dehumanize people". It requires "radical structural changes in mental attitudes and in society" which will "help the poor and disenfranchised gain social, political, and economic power in order to have an effective voice and visible presence in the decisions which affect their own lives".

This is not a way of describing the Church's mission which commends itself universally to Episcopalians. Nearly five years ago we launched, nationally, a program for the empowerment, financially, of minority community groups which, even now, is still highly controversial. Many people are more incensed about that program than their fathers were at the discovery that Franklin Roosevelt was an Episcopalian. Without being defensive about the program itself, which is certainly not immune to human imperfections, my concern is the heartbreaking struggle to reach an understanding of Mission which not only can take seriously the agonizing problems of empowerment in our society as an agenda for Christian obedience to Mission but also can provide the full vision of what God is up to in our world. Only such a vision will keep our response in mission from being simply fashionable secular idealism. I am quite ready to say that empowerment is an urgent and critical issue for Christians. It is, and no Christian missionary program is valid in our time which does not confront the problem of the disenfranchised squarely. But empowerment is equally an issue for any citizen in our society. I do not scorn my secular contemporaries if I quote St. Matthew: "Do not even the publicans the same?" I rejoice to walk with anyone, of any faith or none, who will walk the way of liberation with me. And if the church, by its example, can awaken and stimulate the conscience of our people about liberation and empowerment, by all means let us do so. But to say that the gaining of social, political, and economic power is in any sense the exhaustive and decisive goal of Christian mission is to say nonsense, and this is often what we seem to say.

Very often those who are troubled by so restrictive a statement or who wish to move beyond it to what might be concerns more peculiarly Christian in their origin are often hard-pressed in their task. If one wishes to broaden our understanding of liberation to include not only the social, political, and economic empowerment which is, after all, part of the universal secular American myth, but to go beyond that to the depths of the Biblical understanding of liberation, he is likely to wind up with apples and oranges. Mission is empowerment of the poor and it is also baptizing people. It is funding community groups and it is also teaching the Creed. Until we can find a statement of mission which can establish the relevance to our brothers in our society of both political clout and Christian conversion and initiation, in the same terms and with the same urgent, salvific bearing on the human situation, we are not likely to move out of our polarization.

Where is such an inclusive statement to be found? My feeling is that the best place to begin is in one's own locality, working with one's neighbors. Broad, general theological formulations of mission may be possible and even useful, but they will have power and reality only as long as they reflect actual experience in mission. The more inclusive the experience, the better will be the reflection on it. This is why I pray for more and more ecumenical action in local situations. And there is, it seems to me, a particular case to plead for emphasis on Anglican-Roman sharing. Here are two churches, each committed to social action, each committed in some degree to empowerment, each also deeply committed to the full range of God's liberating action in the gospel. Let those congregations in their own communities begin to work in mission together, together serving in common action, together reflecting on the relationship between that action in society and the other action they also take, of prayer and sacrament and worship and self-discipline. Is it not possible — indeed has not experience already proved? — that out of such fruitful, local collaboration new learning will come which will move us out of our polarized paralysis? I do not know what the Roman Catholic Church needs in its understanding of mission but I can well see the unifying power of such experience from the Episcopalian point of view — see it and covet it. The future will take little account of either activism or pietism when they are put forward separately as alternative styles of churches and mission.

Another seminal area is that of theological statement and teaching. The Anglican way of learning and teaching theology has generally been the liturgical way: *lex orandi lex credendi* is a principle traditionally dear to us, and the Prayer Book has been our main vehicle for this teaching. It was an admirable way to guard and teach the Tradition, to pray our theology and to cleanse and deepen our prayer. It was also a perilous way for it tended to breed a carelessness within Anglicanism, a sometimes-frivolous feeling that we did not need to engage in the hard work of theological exploration and could remain loftily aloof about confessional formularies and disputes. We were not a confessional body; we had no positions of our own; we had no founder, no *Summa*, no Trent. Our little catechism was an essay in personal identity, beginning "What is your name?" and issuing in brief statements of what Anglicans are to do. The 39 Articles were an interesting historical exhibit of how far an Anglican could go toward being a Presbyterian without being one. The creeds, the Scriptures, the two major sacraments, the apostolic ministry — those were enough.

At its best, this general position was a blessing. It saved us from much unfruitful theological squabbling and nourished a liberal and tolerant spirit which could beget even holiness, as in an Andrewes or a Gore. It could also, and did, breed a spirit of indifferentism, of formalism, which was destructive of any growth in Christ. Now, in our time, it is no longer a tenable position, mainly on two grounds.

First, the Prayer Book as a single coherent entity is not likely to be a functioning reality — at least during the foreseeable future of liturgical experiment and revision. We shall have a variety of rites and a far less restricted array of prayers, and while this new freedom may very well enrich and quicken our liturgical life it will also sharply limit the usefulness of the Prayer Book as teacher, conservator and transmitter of the Church's faith.

Second, the Anglican distaste for confessional theology is by now hopelessly passé. It is a luxury the Church in our time cannot afford. Man in contemporary society faces issues of social order, of conscience, of identity, of meaning with which he cannot cope by merely traditional statements. Great as is the danger of an attractive new confession being a terrible pseudo-solution for him, there is a greater danger in saying nothing to him except what has been hallowed and has become treasured over the years. The Anglican attitude has often been that of a free-loader on what others have done — a kind of eclecticism which disdained the hard confessional work but used the fragments which fell from the confessional table.

But this is no longer possible. Neither Rome nor classical Protestantism any longer provides the fixed points they once did which helped so much to locate Anglicanism. And when we can no longer define ourselves simply as different from something else and must make our own statement, we are suddenly aware of our need for and our inexperience in the confessional/theological task. A year ago at an (Anglican) theological colloquium, Fr. John Ford quoted a scientist-friend's observation that "the real advancement in scientific inquiry comes when there is a conceptual crisis — when a concept, so to speak, has to turn in on itself, to reflect upon itself, and then hopefully something new and vital can emerge". Fr. Ford went on to say, "It just struck me that there may be an ecumenical equivalent to this. In other words, when one reaches a confessional crisis, this of course is dismaying, causes anguish, may be exasperating, frutrating, and so on. But it also may be the human means for advancement". This is something Anglicanism needs to learn.

This is, in a way, the province of ARC, and their method. But they need have no copyright on it. The confessional crises are everywhere — in seminaries, in consortia for social action, in youth's attempts to come to grips with personal realities, wherever old confessions have broken down. It is in precisely those areas that Anglicans need experience and increasingly find it. For the future I can see, part of the ecumenical task must be that of framing "confessions" of a new kind and variety. At the same colloquium I mentioned earlier, one of the Anglican members had this to say about the need of the Episcopal Church to come to terms with other ways of formulating and expressing the faith than merely the great credal or sacerdotal symbols:

> This statement (The C.O.C.U. Plan's earlier chapters) — and similar ones today, including many by Vatican II — are designed to unite, to serve as a basis of unity. Many earlier confessions were designed in part to divide, to separate heretics out and drive them out! The whole purpose of modern confessions is basically different and, as long as the statement is unifying and does preserve the paradoxes and differences of emphasis — Episcopalians need not be uneasy.

I would add two brief qualifiers. I would add "mystery" to what must be preserved, and I would put the Episcopalian stance in positive terms. It is not that we need not fear; it is rather that we should be eagerly welcome. It is this unifying task, fruitful of such confessional statements as those on Eucharist and the like, which ARC and ARCIC have pioneered, which are models for many areas and levels of our two churches' approach to unity.

The third and fourth areas I mention more briefly. The third area is that of authority. I am reluctant to enter into the great issues of Biblical authority or of infallibility and indefectibility. Anglican churches have con-

29

tented themselves with accepting Scripture as the test of doctrine without going into the finer questions of literal prescription and the like. And Anglicanism has never claimed infallibility for its authorities. It has only claimed to be right, with the corollary that it was open to being proved wrong in the next test of reasonable thought. These are great issues, with much yet to be thought and explored.

I would speak of authority in two more manageable contexts — authority in ministry and authority in moral standards. It would be pleasant to think that Anglican patterns in church government and those now being explored within the Roman Church are much the same. I'm not sure this is so. In some aspects of collegiality, Anglicans have retained or achieved useful norms, as in the modest teaching authority vested in the House of Bishops, say, or the autonomous character of the Episcopalian priesthood in a vote by orders in the General Convention. But these evidences of collegiality are far from telling the whole story. There is a diocesanism as well as a parochialism which sometimes become destructive factors in Anglican life. The diocese is, no doubt, the smallest complete expression of the Church. But the Church is not a mere confederation of dioceses; it is, in its full mystery, a body whose smallest model is the faithful clergy and laity gathered around their bishop but whose fulness far exceeds any such unit or any federation of units. And Anglican church government, especially in the younger churches and countries, inadequately represents that.

For another instance, I would say that the participation by lay persons at every level of church government — much though I welcome that and give thanks for it —

is far from the ideal of corporate life which Christians should seek. The long tradition of professional priesthood and the inheritance of clerical privilege and protection tend to excite in our laity both belligerence and timidity—a belligerence as of one caste against another, a timidity, a fear as of people afraid to touch holy things or enter holy places. This is a long way from collegiality, and it is a long way from any deep understanding of the single, universal priesthood of Christ exercised through the royal priesthood of His people. And I take it that only such fresh understanding can provide Anglicans or Romans with the renewed and ordered authority in ministry we seek.

In this search, it may be that both churches start on an even footing. Each may find in the other elements of renewing insight without any impulse to mere imitation, and each may assist the other to perceive the under-used and unrecognized values hidden in our separate traditions of government. But this must not be simply an exercise in comparative ecclesiology. The end is not to be more familiar and confident friends. The end is to be one household and one bread, with no more variation than becomes two sons of one father.

Authority in moral standards is a far more complex matter, and I touch on only the most elementary aspects of it. It would be folly to suppose that any church — much less two — can arrive at a single, comprehensive moral theology in this time in history. I say this not in helpless resignation but in recognition of the fact that one does not write a manual of military strategy in the middle of a battle. The battle, so to speak, is everywhere around us. That is to say that humanity has never had to confront so bewildering an array of choices that must be made — decisions about social and political structure, empowerment, environment, sexuality, genetic manipulation, the right to die, the right to be born, racism, nationalism, education . . . where would the list stop? So broad and subtly-changing a frontier makes systematic analysis almost impossibly difficult, and the ceaseless flood of new data and new possibilities induces in moralists the greatest caution.

Yet men and women must choose. We may be, as one Episcopal philosopher observed, "morally responsible and intellectually incompetent", but that does not lift from man's shoulders the burden of saying yes or no. It only means that we must make our choices and establish our lines with the best wisdom we can muster and in company with as many other Christians as we can. For all that many specialized task groups are doing in this area, there is still much more to be done in the way of ecumenical study — in all sorts of groups — and the adoption of common lines of action and common standards of witness. The question of abortion is not a Roman Catholic problem no matter what the *New York Times* may think, nor is the environmental irresponsibility of a large corporation reserved to the National Council of Churches.

It strikes me that one of the most productive sorts of ecumenical encounter is that which takes place around a public issue. Quite apart from the significance of the issue itself and the need for informed Christian judgment on it, it is the nature of that kind of encounter to move the participating churches away from defensiveness or narcissism and back to the great sources of Christian judgment. This is uniting in its spirit, and can open new learnings to all who share it.

Last of all, I instance the life of prayer and the ascetical disciplines as an area where the future presses on us with singular intensity. The extraordinary religiosity of even the ecclesiastically alienated is notable. The bleak landscape of our society frightens many of us, young and old, and we seek comfort and assurance from any sort of experience which can be deemed transcendental. The dangers in this vast homesickness are obvious — retreat from confrontation, retreat from action, morbid self-indulgence and all the rest of it. But such diagnosis, however accurate, does not do away with the problem. The problem, as I think Christians would put it, is that of redressing the balance of our life so that the whole range of Divine action and liberation will be steadily remembered.

There is a solitude in prayer, a necessary solitude, but it is not a retreat into remote loneliness; it is rather the inner silence of the intense concentration of a man fighting for his life. There is an expectant waiting in prayer but it is not mere passivity or resignation; it is a necessary response of dialogue. So one could continue identifying elements which are well-nigh universal in all prayer, yet which are filled with particular meanings, new and old, drawn from Christian understandings of God's way with man. The distinctive elements in Christian prayer, in other words, are not generally activities or forms; they are rather the ways in which Christian faith and Biblical insight informs and uses the multitude of ways in which man approaches and contemplates reality.

What is needed is not discussion of prayer, but praying, if the Christian community is to respond adequately to the obvious hunger of so many of our contemporaries for some effective and credible experience of a mystical

33

apprehension of reality. If we are to be rescued from pietistic retreat from encounter with reality or magical attempts to manipulate it, the only way is in a new commitment to the steady practice of prayer. There is no reason in the world for this to be anything other than an ecumenical enterprise from the beginning. I have mentioned four areas where the future presses strongly on the present and where I think significant contours for tomorrow are to be found. Our understanding of Mission will be a major determinant of the form and work of the Church that lies ahead. Renewal in confessional theology and a fresh hold on the authority of ministry will profoundly affect our capacity to respond in mission. Renewal in our life of prayer will open the door to the power of the Spirit to fulfill our offering and our commitment and empower our capacities. These are to me the significant areas for mutual exploration in the ecumenical dialogue of our two churches. I claim nothing more for them than that they seem to me fertile and exciting, from my perch among the grassroots.

I close with three brief comments, or rather questions. ARC and ARCIC rightfully take the lead in particular salients of strategic importance. But is there any level of the two churches' life where dialogue and common study and work should not take place — among seminarians, local groups of clergy, families in a neighborhood, congregations sharing a community or whatever? I know of none — indeed I know of few where such things are not already taking place.

If, as I would hope, some special emphasis is to be laid on work in the four fields I mention, how shall that be done without violence to the ecumenical rubrics which seem to me so important? How can encouragement be given to the deeper exploration of empowerment, say, or the search for new models of authority in ministry without running the risk of paralyzing local initiatives, or bypassing the possibility of learning by some bureaucratic appearance of knowing the answer already? Perhaps all we could do would be to recruit some extraordinary observers who could hear and see what is going on and somehow encourage it without endangering it. I don't know how that will be.

What is our motivation in all this exploration? Sometimes it is said to be a search for strength — the hang-together syndrome. I question the validity of that. In yesterday's newspaper we read of the anticipated disappearance of the Roman Catholic Church in the United States in 20 years. I have heard similar predictions about the Episcopal Church. If what was meant by those predictions was such radical changes in both churches that they would be unrecognizable, I might be prepared to accept the prediction — even welcome it. But I'm afraid what was meant was not that kind of growth in grace but simply the extinguishing, by death, of any constituency at all. I do not believe this and it does not motivate me at all.

I am not afraid that there won't be any churches left. I am afraid of the kind of churches ours might be, if we are not true to our ecumenical vocation. The motivation which matters is not fear of extinction, it is fear of unfaithfulness to the greatness of what has been given us. The time perhaps was when loyalty to truth seemed to require separateness. If that was so, I do not question the gifts that God made to each of us, in our separateness. But it is kindergarten wisdom to know that that time has passed and that even what we have will be taken from us, if we do not move toward unity, and that all we shall have left is the bitter fruit of separateness from one another and from our history. That bitter harvest is precisely what could produce perfectly viable and prosperous churches. That is what I mean by being afraid of the kind of churches ours might be — monuments of meaningless and withdrawn pietism. In God's mercy we can be spared that if we take counsel not of our fears or cautious diplomacy but only of our unity in Christ Jesus to whom be the glory now and forever.

II

DOCTRINAL AGREEMENT

Doctrinal Agreement in The Church

by
ARTHUR A. VOGEL

SUMMARY

Faith, community, language, and common experience are interrelated. The relation of *the* world all men share to the many subworlds men elaborate for themselves throws light on the relation of the church to the many churches. A "pilgrim church" and its religious language are both "on the way"; a personal presence which transcends language is the source of religious language's authenticity. Common acceptance of the baptismal faith and substantial agreement on the nature of sacraments would be sufficient to enable Christians to recognize each other's churches as rooms of their Father's house (John 14:2), thus enabling them to be at home with each other.

Properly understood, a search for agreement on faith is a search for community.

That should not surprise us, for "the" faith is always a statement made by a community, and, as a statement, it is expressed in language. Languages belong to communities, for no man owns a language. Statements of faith are produced within communities and depend on the common experience of communities. Meaning and community are fundamentally coextensive, for both grow out of shared experience. Such facts as we are mentioning justify our opening contention that search for agreement on faith is search for community, but, that fact notwithstanding, men may search for agreement on faith in ways which keep community from developing. Meaning grows out of common experience, but as soon as meaning is expressed in statements, the verbal expression of the statements can be removed from the experience which produced them. So removed from the experiential matrix in which they arose, statements can abstractly be put together in a way which threatens community instead of expressing it. That is the fear many people have of "unity negotiations."

The problem addressed by the ecumenical search for agreement on faith is how, through statements which necessarily abstract from experience, Christians can move to a common experience which will so found their lives that they can sacramentally celebrate their oneness in Christ together.

Four prerequisites, I suggest, are necessary for the successful resolution of that problem:

I.   A recognition of the basic problem for what it is, one manifesting itself beyond the bounds of religion narrowly conceived.

II.   We must recognize the need for a religion as large as reality and not live provincial religious lives. We must neither knowingly nor unknowingly worship a god who is "too small," who can only work in one area of reality in one way. Christians worship the true creator God, the God who sustains the cosmos and who offers a cosmic recreation in Christ. That God can speak to us in all ways, not just in one way, for all creation is his language.

III.   Since God chose to redeem man by entering the

world through the incarnation of the Father's Word, Christians must recognize that the structure of the Word has been incorporated into the structure of their new lives in Christ: into recreation, redemption, grace, the sacraments, and the church. Recent emphasis on the pilgrim nature of the church, the importance of the human body for understanding the sacraments, the communal nature of grace, and the historical and cultural relativity of human expression are important.

IV. We must recognize, as a result of the first three points, that there is a sense in which the world is the model for the church; the church is not a completely self-contained model for the world. The grace committed to the church is meant to be the source of a "new world"; that world, as God's Kingdom, must ultimately coincide with all men and all creation.

Those prerequisites accepted, we can discover a new way to ask the question about the measure of doctrinal agreement necessary for the unity of the church. It is by way of a more general question about the relation of diversity to unity at large: what kind of diversity enriches our world? What kind of diversity fragments it?

Asking the ecumenical question in those terms indicates that the religious problem is not unique. We discover it other places, and there is a sense in which we discover it other places *first*. Until we recognize how widespread a problem is, we will not be able to solve it, for we will not truly recognize *it*. If a new way of asking a question reveals that the question is larger than we thought, ways of dealing with it in other areas may lead us to new answers in more restricted areas.

We have now asked the question about doctrinal unity within the church in terms as general as our experience of the world itself. Examining our personal experience in the world, is it not true to say that in one sense all human beings live in one world, while in another sense they live in many different worlds? How can we account for that unity and diversity? To what do we refer when we speak of living in one world, and to what do we refer when we speak of living in different worlds?

To say that all men live in one world, a world bigger than that which receives them into itself, is a way of saying all men share an over-arching, common experience. What? Of being limited in their existence. The one context all men share — and so the oneness of their common world which cannot be lost — is that of not calling themselves into being. In their birth and death all men are passive and receptive. Finitude is a "structure," or "horizon" permeating (and so unifying) everything human. While alive, proud men may psychologically try to deny their finitude, playing god, but even proud men die. Death ends psychological games and reasserts the primal unity of the human world.

Although the finitude of our lives defines a common world-context shared by all men, as embodied persons, we develop different perspectives within that world. We see things differently within the common horizon of finitude. In our different communities (for example, in our families, schools, professional groups, cultural groups, etc.), we positively develop different perspectives or ways of viewing reality; these perspectives account for the fact that people live in "different worlds" within one common world. We construct many partial worlds of meaning in community with each other.

The difference between the oneness of our common world and the plurality of our partial worlds is marked by the fact that the unifying horizon of our one world is something over which we have no control, while we ourselves actively create the different world views which emerge within that horizon. Our common condition of finitude precedes all of our choices as their condition, while the many worlds we elaborate during our lives primarily result from our choices. Our common world is the condition of our specialized worlds, but the satisfaction we derive from actively making our specialized worlds draws our attention away from the unifying structure of our being over which we have no choice. War, strife, conflict, suspicion, aggression, defensiveness result when the plurality of human worlds is allowed to eclipse the oneness of man's common world. Due to each man's ambition and preoccupation with himself, he tries to act as if his subworld was *the* world. Again men try to play god, and the history of the world as we know it results.

Plurality in unity is the human condition. That condition was reasserted by the Father who first created it when he sent his Son into the world at a certain time and place in history. The dynamic structure of human life was not destroyed, but perfected, by the new creation God instituted in Jesus Christ. God always creates a uni-verse. Consequently the dynamic tension of plurality in unity will be found within the church and Kingdom as well as in the first creation they perfect. Only so can the richness and variety of the Father's infinite goodness be shown; only so can finite beings most fully mirror the perfection of God.

It is time now more specifically to turn our attention to the structure of the church. At the moment we do not find the church as the Father wants it to be; that is why the church is said always to need reformation and that is

41

why Christians are presently engaged in the ecumenical movement.

We suggest there is an analogy between the one world and the many worlds of man and the oneness of God's church and the many churches presently existing within it. The same tension, it would appear, is found within the church at large as is found within the world at large. Let us develop the ecclesial side of the analogy further.

Christians believe all men are saved through Jesus Christ, by being incorporated into the new creation begun in him. The singleness of man's dependence on the Christ is shown by the singleness of baptism and the oneness of the body St. Paul says Christians enter through baptism. Christ has but one body, and the church, his mystical body in the world, must be one also.

As our finitude and our dependence upon a reality beyond us structure the oneness of *the* human world, so *that* finitude and dependence is further specified and revealed by God's love for us in Jesus Christ. In both our creation (by which we enter the one human world) and our recreation (by which we become members of the one body of Christ) our oneness is manifested by the fact that we *receive* the gift of life (new life) from another. In each case we receive the conditions within which all of our activities take place. Unity, then, both in the world and in the church, is something we receive; it is found where God's oneness and primacy are obvious.

Incorporated into Christ through baptism, however, we, at the same time, enter different communities of men, who, due to the fact they are embodied persons, develop perspectively different lives within the "new life" of Jesus Christ. Such communal orientations within Christianity are merely manifestations within religion of the way man orients himself within the world at large. Due to their finiteness, men must be perspectives.

The unfortunate thing is that the perversions we see in the world at large are also found in religion, and in the latter case they are apt to be proposed in the name of God himself. In religion, too, men play god.

Living together in ecclesial communities we creatively elaborate styles of life that effectively enable us to live in "different worlds." Within our ecclesial communities, as in all subworlds, our activities tend to make us forget our finitude. We forget (or give only formal recognition to) the Father's gift to us in Christ in favor of our elaboration and use of that gift. Stated in terms of our previous analysis: we forget *the* world because of our over-involvement in *our* world.

Flushed by the activity involved in elaborating our theologies and our theories, we forget the limited nature our language has in the first place. Concerned with God, the Absolute, we feel his absoluteness guarantees our language about him. When that happens, theological discussion among individuals and churches becomes a confrontation of absolutes — but all within the context of finitude! We must remember that even when grace is operative it does not universalize man.

The solution to the ecumenical problem would be found if Christians could learn to structure and elaborate their on-going communal lives in such a way that the Father's primacy — his gift to man in Christ and the Spirit — was their obvious theme. If *the* Christian world centering in the gift to men of Christ's body obviously ordered the Christian perspectives originating in men's bodies, the church would have the unity in the midst of diversity God intended for it. It would be a grace-ful uni-verse.

At this point the reader may say, "Well enough; the analysis and analogy are sound, but they are general. How do we go about making actual progress?" We would go a long way toward the achievement of our goal if we better understood the nature of language and the growth of human consciousness.

Obviously we cannot give a detailed analysis of these topics here, but consensus is evolving out of such a vast number of studies and inquiries on these subjects that perhaps prolonged analysis is not needed.

Contemporary studies show that it is not too much to say that man's mode of existence is dialogical. Human consciousness grows through others; the first attitude a child must develop in the world is that of trust in another, for he is completely dependent on others in his being. Reciprocal relations with other persons is prior to our knowledge of material things in the world; again the life of an infant in relation to those who care for him — his family or a family substitute — furnishes a convincing illustration. We know other persons before we know things, and we know things through persons. Our first perceptions are of other persons, and such perception ultimately reveals that we are known before we know and that we are loved before we love.

We have previously mentioned that language, the means by which we can most completely express ourselves and the world, is itself communal. Progress in science and knowledge in general depends on dialogue and community: thus we see the need for professional societies, journals, and meetings.

None of this surprises a Christian who believes in the

44

Trinity, for his God is himself a community of Persons, a dialogue of presence, of knowing, of loving, and of giving. A "pilgrim church" is a church "on the way," and so is necessarily engaged in dialogue. The church is a community of persons growing through their reciprocal relations with God, each other, and all men.

We must take these facts seriously! Being "on the way" is a characteristic of everything in the world; it is a feature of the oneness of our world. Religious language, as our lives and as the church itself, is "on the way." No language is adequate to God. God is not an object, fixed before man, to be examined, and about which objective tests can be given. God meets man in the all-engulfing mystery of personal presence, and religion is life in that presence, not formal propositions about that presence.

God can be recognized at any moment of the world's history only because of his presence. For Christians, the presence of God is the essence of time, which explains why vestiges of the past should not control the present. Linguistic expressions used in the past could not control the presence of God even when that past was the present, all the less now. Still, the presence of God has continued throughout history, and recognition of that constancy should show in our religious expression. Because language is always furnished to us by the communities into which we are born and because such language sediments the lived experience of previous generations, an important dimension of Christian language is remembering. (In the constancy of God's presence, the past Christians remember is the basis of their hope for the future.) Christian language and expression, then, never start afresh, for they are a continuing response to the presence of but one God in history. The oneness of God's presence

45

in every present that is now past must show in our response to him, if our response is to *him* in the way he works in history.

The "content" of Christian revelation is the presence of a Person. Such presence can only be known in expression, but the presence itself is always more than any expression of it. Language between persons becomes authentic when a presence which lives beyond it speaks through it in a present. It is in actual use, in other words, that religious language — language between persons — becomes authentic. Speaking to us in the present, God always calls us into a future which is new; for in every "now" his presence is more than we have known, more than we have expressed, and more than we can know. His presence for us is always mission into the future as whole men with all men.

Under the judgment of God's presence, formal statements alone cannot test or determine a person's "orthodoxy." Orthodoxy is not the possession of an intellectual content; it is a commitment, in trust, to the Person who is Word. Texts of the Christian Bible and Creeds are not their own content. The presence of a Person is the content of Scripture and of theological formulations, not certain words or passages from the texts themselves. That is why the church is fittingly the "sacrament of dialogue": it is the means of bringing people into each other's presence and into the presence of God. In such presence is found both growth and a manifestation in the world of the intimate life of the Trinity.

Authentic language in religion is language "on the way," i.e., in processes of revealing God's presence. Language can never adequately *represent* God; instead it is a means by which God's presence rules us. In truly religious language God always makes us new through a personal involvement, calling us beyond ourselves. Authentic religious language does not present something external to us with which we have no involvement, and upon which we have no dependence, and then ask us to make a judgment about that thing while remaining exactly as we are.

Understanding the limited nature of religious language for what it is, is a way of recognizing the primacy of *the* Christian world given to us by grace over the elaborations of men within that world. Where we live is our home. If we live only in the subworld our community makes, the subworlds other communities make will threaten us. If, on the other hand, we live more consciously in the oneness of God's gift to us in Christ — in the new creation in which all men must admit their total dependence on God—then we will feel that *God's world*, the one body of Christ, is our home; the "worlds" other men make can then be seen as rooms of one home. In that way the words of Jesus Christ can become a proclamation to the world: "In my Father's house are many rooms . . ." (John 14:2). Acknowledging the primacy of God is the only way men can be at home with each other.

The question for Christian unity newly asked is: "Are human subworlds (the churches) enriching dimensions of the *one new creation* all men have in Christ?" "Creation," we must understand, is not used in Christian theology to describe *how* God made the universe; it is rather the statement *that* all positive reality outside of God depends completely on God. "Creation" means "complete dependence." To judge churches by the way they manifest their *complete* dependence on God, would minimize the use of abstract "tests" by men of each other from

47

their limited points of view. Mission in the world, a community's life-orientation, basic attitudes, would become more important. To acknowledge one's dependence on God makes one more open to others; thus dialogue with all men and the world would be seen to constitute the life of the church, instead of being an option the church may or may not choose to exercise. The life of the Trinity revealed in Christ's giving himself to others would then show more obviously both to those within and outside the church. In that way, Christians, growing in community through shared experience, would be constantly discovering new truths about God in his overriding presence. They would be intent on gracefully trying to actualize God's promises for the future in the present, instead of trying to "protect the past" and allowing it to override the present. Mission to the world would be emphasized in the church's life.

Still, we must *think* about what is important to us, and our actions should be thoughtful, meaningful ones. There must be theology, and there must be creedal proclamations. The only question is what their role should be. Our suggestion is that there should be one mode of testimony that we have *knowingly received God's gift* of himself in Christ through the Spirit. The father gives us a covenant relationship (New Testament) with him in Christ. He sends his Word to say something, and we should be explicit about what we hear and about what our response is in faith. But the emphasis should be on what God is and does for us.

Life in Christ is our recreation; that recreation (redemption) is our new mode of recognizing our finitude, our total dependence on God. The covenanted way of entering the new creation and becoming a member of

Christ's mystical body is through baptism. The condition of death to self and life with God effected in baptism describes the new "common world" all men enter as Christians. The baptismal faith traditionally set forth in the baptismal creed(s) should be the sufficient agreement in faith for men mutually to acknowledge their existence in one church.

However, coincident with entering the *one* world, whether it be the "natural world" of our first birth or the new world of our rebirth in Christ, we have seen that we necessarily enter subworlds, the pluralistic worlds made by different communities of men. If Christians are to live full lives together within the one church, their communal subworlds must be positively and cooperatively oriented towards each other within the primacy of their common dependence on Jesus Christ.

The way different Christian communities show their inclusion within God's new creation, while consciously elaborating subworlds (*typoi*) which are peculiar to them, is through the sacramental structure of the church. The sacraments are the way men cooperate with God in their local communities in his on-going creation of the new world — the "building up of the body." Sacraments are the matrix within which the daily lives of Christians are lived and their daily decisions made.

If men cannot agree on the meaning and nature of the sacraments — especially on Christian initiation, the eucharist, ministry, and marriage — they will be consciously opposing each other in what is meant to be their cooperative, daily activity. Paradoxical as it may sound, fundamental statements of faith rehearsing the mighty acts of God and our dependence on him are too easy to make. Fundamentals are always hard to deny: who denies death at a funeral? Our daily worlds are the fields of many little things, and it is in the countless "little decisions" we make throughout the day that our personal attitudes most reveal themselves. That is one reason why the people with whom we share our daily worlds become our most intimate friends: they are the people with whom we have most in common. Unity is the sharing of something common. At the level of our daily lives — in our sacramental lives, in other words — Christian unity must also manifest itself.

Until there is thoughtful, i.e., theological, agreement on the substantial nature of the sacraments and sacramental living there can be no effective Christian unity in the world. Substantial agreement is not the same thing as full agreement, but it is enabling agreement. It would enable the mission of the church obviously to be sustained by the one sacramental bread of life, and it would establish a common experiential context within which Christians could grow together in their discovery of God's truth.

The church is itself a sacrament; its basic unity must be sacramental also. That fact should be recognized by faith. To find churches which live, in doctrinal understanding, substantially the same sacramental lives within the one baptismal faith of total dependence on the Father in the Son by the Spirit is to discover the essential unity of the church amidst the necessary plurality of men. Agreement in *the* faith need state no more than that.

Reflections on Doctrinal Agreement

by
AVERY DULLES, S.J.

SUMMARY

How can the divided churches of our day overcome their inherited disagreements and grant each other full recognition as communities of Christian faith? This paper concentrates on four theological principles which may be helpful for this goal: systematic pluralism, historical consciousness, sociocultural adaptation, and mutual receptivity. The conclusion is that even in cases where fully satisfactory consensus statements cannot be achieved, churches may be able at times to recognize the legitimacy of one another's doctrinal formulations.

Necessity of Doctrinal Agreement

The Anglican-Roman Catholic Consultation in the United States, at its December 1969 meeting, declared that organic unity, while hard to visualize in its particulars, would necessarily include, among other things, "a common profession of faith."[1] Why should this be necessary? If the Church were simply a communion of love, doctrinal agreement might be superfluous. It might be enough for the members of the Church, despite their intellectual differences, to be bound to one another by friendship and mutual concern. The Church, however, understands itself as a community of faith and witness, called into being by public revelation. In order to exist as *such* a community it must find ways by which its members can recognize one another as responding to the

51

same self-disclosure of God in Jesus Christ and as being committed to a common life of witness, worship, and service.

Among the various means whereby the Church articulates its faith and commitment, language has been found the least ambiguous. Individuals and groups who can sincerely join in the same confession of faith are thought to have fulfilled one of the necessary conditions for membership in the same body. Conversely those who cannot conscientiously take part in such professions of faith are commonly judged not to belong to the same religious community. Thus language is used in a discriminative way to identify true believers.

The discriminative use of language may be observed on two distinct levels, rather imprecisely distinguishable from each other. The first level is that of proclamation. Acceptance of the basic kerygma concerning Jesus as the crucified and risen Lord is generally taken as the principal criterion distinguishing Christians from non-Christians. The second level is that of doctrine or interpretation. Conceivably the Church might allow complete freedom for its members to hold whatever views they personally regard as compatible with the basic proclamation; but in point of fact the Church has from the beginning maintained that certain doctrinal stands should not be tolerated within the community. In the Epistles of the New Testament we find severe condemnations of the views of judaizers, antinomians, gnostics, and others. Paul was especially harsh on ideas that led to scandalous or uncharitable conduct.

As a result of its insistence on right doctrine, Christianity, like many other ideological groups, has become internally divided into mutually antagonistic parties.

While Christians of different factions are at one in their commitment to the basic proclamation, they are opposed in that they reject one another's interpretations of that proclamation.

Extent of Necessary Agreement

Not all doctrinal differences are divisive of the Christian community. Opinions that are recondite, tentative, peripheral to the gospel, or lacking in practical import are frequently tolerated, even by groups that firmly reject them. There are no clear objective criteria for distinguishing between tolerable and intolerable errors. Following their best judgment, some churches have adopted a kind of integralism[2] that would regard almost nothing as negotiable, whereas others, at the opposite end of the spectrum, have attempted to single out a small number of "fundamentals" or "necessary doctrines."[3] Sociological investigation might be able to throw light on the reasons for varying degrees of severity or liberality in doctrinal matters.

For most contemporary Christians it is surprising to see how much importance the Church has at times attached to relatively abstruse and apparently inconsequential doctrines. This was true in the Byzantine Church at the end of the Patristic era and again in the Western Church in the high middle ages, when subtle points about the Trinitarian processions, the beatific vision, and the fires of purgatory were debated with astonishing self-assurance.

Although time does not automatically heal all wounds, we need not assume that Christians are condemned to live forever under the accumulated weight of all their past disagreements. It may be possible to transcend the painful dilemma of a choice between integralism and fundamentalism. Our age, I believe, offers many new resources for re-establishing the acknowledged unity of faith without infidelity to venerated traditions and at the same time without capitulation to formulas now perceived to be inept. These new resources for present purposes may be grouped under four headings: systematic pluralism, historical consciousness, sociocultural adaptation, and mutual receptivity.

Systematic Pluralism

Until recently the prevalent theological mentality has been deeply marked by the objectivism of Greco-Roman metaphysics. The concepts and terms of theology were presumed to correspond, one to one, to realities of the supernatural order. But the new pluralism is not wholly unprecedented. As early as the fifth century it began to force its way into ecclesiastical teaching. The conflict between Alexandrian and Antiochian Christology perhaps provides the clearest illustration from the Patristic age.[4] Cyril of Alexandria, whose personal theology clearly appeared in his celebrated anathemas against Nestorious (430), was compelled by the exigencies of the situation to allow the legitimacy of the "two natures" doctrine in the Formula of Union (433), thus paving the way for the adoption of that doctrine at Chalcedon (451). On the other hand, even after Chalcedon, Cyril's own preferred formula, "the one incarnate nature of the Word of God," continued to be tolerated in the Church. The Lateran Council of 649, in one canon, accepted the doctrine of those who confess, "according to the Fathers," that there is "one incarnate nature of the divine

Word," provided that they in no way compromise the perfection of Christ's humanity. In the next canon the Council approved of those who say, "according to the Fathers," that Christ is "of and in two natures substantially united but distinct and undivided."[5] In these two canons, taken together, the pluralism of systems is implicitly acknowledged. While the position of Eutyches is condemned, that of Cyril of Alexandria, who uses similar terminology, is not. While the position of Nestorius is condemned, that of John of Antioch, who uses similar terminology, is not. The decisive thing is not the terminology, which has different meanings in different systems, but rather the faith, which is to be differently expressed according to the system adopted.

Because of the persistence of Greek metaphysical objectivism, the pluralism of systems has only with great difficulty gained acceptance. The diversity of schools in medieval theology is not a genuine pluralism because, as Rahner points out, these schools generally operated within a common intellectual horizon; they were thought to agree about essentials and to differ only with regard to certain marginal questions.[6] The principle of comprehensiveness, as understood in the Anglican tradition, perhaps comes closer to the present-day concept of systematic pluralism. Through its historic controversies the Church of England learned to be very slow to condemn expressions that might be difficult to reconcile with orthodox formulations. "It has been the tradition of Anglicanism to contain within one body both Protestant and Catholic elements. But there is a continuing search for the whole truth in which these elements will find complete reconciliation. Comprehensiveness implies a willingness to allow liberty of interpretation, with a certain slowness in arresting or restraining exploratory thinking."[7]

In the twentieth century, doctrinal pluralism has come into its own, thanks, in part, to the careful attention given to the peculiarities of religious language. It is widely recognized today that faith has to do with mystery and therefore cannot be embodied, without remainder, in clear concepts and formulas. Religious language necessarily relies on analogous terms abstracted from man's ordinary experience of the world about him. Each analogy has its limitations, and therefore the full truth is best approached, in many instances, through a variety of paradigms or models, which mutually offset one another's defects but which are incapable, even jointly, of affording a univocal formula that fully comprehends the truth of revelation.

As theology comes to recognize the legitimacy of irreducibly diverse ways of speaking about the same mystery, the coexistence in one and the same Church of multiple theological systems appears, at least potentially, as a positive help for the deeper penetration of revealed truth. Once this is acknowledged, the question of doctrinal differences among the confessions appears in a radically new light. The question is no longer: Can the views of Aquinas, Luther, Calvin, Hooker and others be integrated into a single coherent system? Obviously they cannot. But rather: Can their views be admitted as valid responses to the Christian revelation as viewed from a given standpoint? Thus the churches today have to grapple seriously with a new theological question. As Karl Rahner puts it, speaking as a Roman Catholic, "What does it mean for ecumenical strivings toward a viable unity of the churches, that a genuine pluralism of theologies both exists and has positive right within the Catholic Church?"[8]

Historical Consciousness

Until the development of modern historical consciousness and its penetration, rather recently, into the lives of the churches, the tendency was to assume that past dogmatic statements represented assured results and would forever retain the force and relevance they possessed at the time of their promulgation. If so, it would be hard indeed for Protestants and Catholics today to get beyond the Reformation impasses. Today, however, it is apparent that ancient formulations, even if entirely valid and proper at the time they were adopted, inevitably bear the imprint of their times and thus retain only a limited, though by no means negligible, value for our time. This is true because of their presuppositions, their thought forms and terminology, and their vital context in the history of the Church.

(a) *Presuppositions.* The authors of ancient ecclesiastical statements, like other authors, usually took for granted what was assumed by men of their times. Many of their historical, scientific, and philosophical assumptions we, for good reason, no longer share. As a consequence, we cannot always accept their conclusions without reservations. For example, many earlier ecclesiastical pronouncements regarding the creation of man, the nature and transmission of original sin, and the like, presuppose a kind and degree of historicity in the early chapters of Genesis that are not conceded by sophisticated theologians today. As a result, certain theological questions that were considered closed a century ago have been reopened. The recent discussion of polygenism and the nature of original sin in Roman Catholicism bears witness to this new openness. It is at the moment hard to predict how far this critical probing may be extended to the New Testament, but there are signs that questions such as that of the virginal conception of Jesus are by no means as securely settled within Roman Catholicism as, a generation ago, they were thought to be. Were the older doctrinal pronouncements on such questions based on an ignorance of the literary forms and sources of the infancy gospels? If so, must we not reopen the questions today?⁹

(b) *Thought Forms and Terminology.* Doctrinal definitions are customarily made in terms of the conceptual structures and vocabulary prevalent in the ecclesiastical thinking of their time. For example, categories such as person, nature, and substance, employed in senses derived from the Greek metaphysical tradition, were the vehicles by which many Trinitarian, Christological and Eucharistic questions were adjudicated in the ancient and medieval Church. Today, when other philosophical options are available, the question is inevitably being asked, how can the ancient faith be restated, if at all, in concepts and terms drawn from modern systems such as process philosophy or personalism? Whenever any such statement is attempted, it will of course have to be carefully evaluated to see whether it adequately safeguards the intentions that lay behind the earlier statements.

(c) *Vital Context.* Normally anathemas have been directed not against isolated propositions taken in the abstract but against sets of concatenated propositions understood as the expression of a school or movement. It would be a mistake, subsequently, to take the individual propositions in isolation and to imagine that no one of them could be asserted in any context without incurring the censure of heresy.[10]

For example, a Synod of Constantinople in A.D. 543 published a long list of anathemas agains the Origenists drawn up, it is said, by the Emperor Justinian. The Synod rejected the teaching that at the general resurrection men will rise with spherical bodies.[11] The proposition was condemned within the context of the Origenist system as a whole. Asserted in another context, this curious piece of eschatological speculation would scarcely merit so severe a censure.

Similarly in the late middle ages the Council of Vienne (1312) condemned a whole series of opinions attributed to Pierre Jean Olivi, a leader of the radical Franciscan spirituals. In this condemnation, it was declared heretical to deny that the rational soul is "per se et essentialiter" the form of the human body.[12] Now that the crisis caused by the Spiritual Franciscans has passed, the condemnation has, I believe, lost its pertinence.

One could perform a useful ecumenical service by investigating the extent to which old anathemas, adopted in the midst of struggles now forgotten, have fallen into desuetude. For example, can one assume that because the doctrine of indulgences was vigorously asserted by by the Council of Trent against Luther, it follows that no one who denies indulgences can ever be in communion with Rome?[13] Or must the Tridentine Decree on Indulgences be interpreted in the context of the Catholicism of the sixteenth century and in reference to the entire Lutheran system with regard to merit and ecclesiastical mediation?

In working toward a possible restoration of communion among separated Christian groups, it is, I believe, imperative to read past doctrinal affirmations with an adequate sense of history. Otherwise one is faced by the dilemma of either being imprisoned by the past or rebelling against it, to the detriment of living tradition. If each Church is faithful to its own tradition but at the same time seeks to transcend the limitations of the past, there is a genuine possibility of moving toward a wider communion without sacrificing the benefits of the consensus already achieved within each of the denominational traditions.

Sociocultural Adaptation

It would be possible to imagine the truth of Christianity as an objective datum to be imposed indifferently on men of all times and places. The tendency of recent theology, however, is to stress the confessional character of dogmatic utterances. The creed, as the primary cradle of dogma, is a living expression of what a given group of believers finds crucially important in the message of the gospel. "The acceptance of common dogma," that is, dogma imposed without regard to time and place, "weakens the existential character of the Church's decisions and replaces it with a formal act of obedience."[14]

In lieu of this static and extrinsicist notion of dogma, Vatican II promoted the idea that every people should be encouraged to express the faith in a manner suited to its native endowments, its history, and its culture.[15] In accordance with the plan of the Incarnation, says the Decree on Missionary Activity, the Church must strive to achieve appropriate expressions of the faith in every major sociocultural area.[16] The Pastoral Constitution on the Church in the Modern World likewise asserts that

60

every nation should develop the ability to express
Christ's message in its own way.[17]

The ecumenical importance of encouraging the diversity of theological styles is brought out by the Decree
on Ecumenism:

> What has been already said about legitimate va-
> riety we are pleased to apply to differences in
> theological expressions of doctrine. In the investi-
> gation of revealed truth East and West have used
> different methods and approaches in understand-
> ing and preaching divine things. It is hardly sur-
> prising, therefore, if sometimes one tradition has
> come nearer than the other to an apt expression
> of certain aspects of the divine mystery, or has
> expressed them in a clearer manner. As a result
> these various theological formulations are to be
> considered as complementary rather than con-
> flicting.[18]

What is here said about the relations between the
Eastern and Western Churches would seem to be appli-
cable, *mutatis mutandis,* to the dialogue among the major confessions in the West. There is every reason to
think that churches that have sunk deep roots into the
culture and history of a given nation or region should
not be required, as a condition for union, to adopt a
foreign style, but should be encouraged to retain and
develop their own characteristic modes of proclamation
and worship. Protestant or Anglican communities in
various countries may in this way assist the correspond-
ing portions of the Roman Catholic population to
achieve styles of thought and expression more consonant
with their natural endowments and cultural heritage,
and in this way to revitalize themselves.

61

The ecumenical situation could be greatly improved if each of the Christian communions would strive to move beyond its historic formulations and to grapple with the urgent questions of our day. Ecumenists may therefore heartily endorse the recommendations of Lambeth 1968 "that theologians be encouraged to continue to explore fresh ways of understanding God's revelation of Himself in Christ, expressed in the language and faith of our time."[19] Authentic modernization may make it possible to transcend many of the ancient polemics, for, as Maurice Wiles has said, "The test of a true development in doctrine is not whether it preserves all the distinctions of the old in their old form; it is whether it continues the objective of the Church in her earlier doctrinal work in a way which is effective and creative in the contemporary world."[20] As more than one author has noted, the goals of renewal and reunion are closely interconnected.[21] One can scarcely hope for reunion except as resulting from a serious effort at renewal.

Mutual Receptivity

Until recently the highest officers or synods of the various denominations had rather firm control of their constituencies. The faithful placed implicit trust in their official leaders and looked to them for decisions as to what the group should think, say, and do. For better or worse, the realities of modern communications have altered this situation. Even within Roman Catholicism, perhaps the most disciplined of the larger denominations, the papacy and the bishops no longer have the power to decide effectively what the people shall believe on controverted points. In the Church as elsewhere, the old authority systems are breaking down. The diaspora situation has replaced the ghetto situation. Christians, while they continue to be strongly influenced by the spokesmen of their own group, do not today give a blank check to their officers. They make up their mind rather on the basis of a total assessment of the evidence.

In this situation it is necessary for denominational authorities to adjust their procedures. They cannot reach decisions peremptorily and unilaterally, as though they could by fiat overcome all contrary opinions. In the present state of Christianity the several magisteria of the divided churches must operate with mutual respect and cooperation; otherwise they may undermine the credibility of their own statements.

Vatican II represented a major step forward, for observer delegates from other Christian bodies were asked to comment on the conciliar texts before these were put into final form by the responsible commissions. At Lambeth in 1968 the official observers from other Christian churches were full, active participants[22] and served as members of the drafting committees. In comparison with these conferences the Roman Catholic episcopal synods of 1967, 1969 and 1971 reflect a regression, for no observer delegates from other communions were invited.

The formula of the future would seem to be a "magisterial mutuality" in which the teaching authorities of the several churches would operate in concert, each recognizing that it does not by itself possess the plenitude of Christian wisdom. Such mutuality does not necessarily presuppose that the churches agree on all points; it makes room for considerable tension and polarity. Mutuality does, however, require that each church should at least listen respectfully to the views of the others and that it should attempt to give the others a rational account of its own position.

Consensus Statements

In closing I should like to make some observations on the role of consensus statements in promoting doctrinal agreements among separated churches. During the past few years many significant consensus statements have been issued by bilateral and multilateral consultations. These statements in my opinion should be encouraged and should be followed up by discussion within the churches. For they may mark out channels through which the churches may ultimately pass. Through common reflection on ecumenically proposed formulas, the several communions may build up a larger fund of common language and theological experience, and thus prepare, on the human level, for the divine gift of future unity.

For maximum utility, consensus statements should meet three conditions. First, they should extend to everything considered essential with regard to the subject matter. If the parties cannot reach agreement on some points regarded as essential, they should specify the remaining area of non-agreement. Secondly, the statements should be viewed as potentially acceptable by the authorities and faithful of the participating churches; otherwise they would scarcely serve to bring the churches themselves together. Finally, they should indicate whether, in the opinions of their authors, the consensus statement represents what must be held, or only what may be held, in each of the communions involved. The fact that the churches can agree positively about what might be said does not suffice for agreement if they disagree about what divergent opinions may also be tolerated.[23]

Is it necessary for doctrinal agreement between churches that their positions be articulated in a consensus statement ratified by both? In view of the analysis of doctrinal pluralism already given, it seems possible that in some instances two churches, without finding it possible to adopt a mutually satisfactory formula, might agree to let each continue to follow its own tradition, provided that certain safeguards are taken to prevent the distortions to which the language of each might be subject. The Council of Florence, in its handling of the *Filioque* question, set an auspicious precedent.[24]

Applying these principles to the Eucharist, one might find that Roman Catholics, seeking to safeguard the real presence and the radical character of the event whereby Christ makes himself present in a reconciling way, might be encouraged to continue to speak, if they choose, of the "sacrifice of the Mass" and of "transubstantiation." On the other hand, Anglicans, or certain groups of Anglicans, might adhere to other expressions that seem to them to do better justice to the uniqueness of Christ's mediatorship and to the mysterious, dynamic nature of the real presence. Each communion, I think, could explain its position in such a way as to do justice to the concerns of the other.

Doctrinal agreement, then, would not necessarily demand a common system of conceptualization and terminology. Without "agreeing to disagree" the churches could allow and even welcome a certain diversity in the theological formulation of the one faith. For as Cardinal Willebrands has said: "None can deny that this unity of faith is indispensable; it is no less sure that diversity of theological approach and explanation is legitimate and can be acknowledged within the unity of faith, and within the Church."[25]

III

LITURGICAL CONVERGENCE

An Anglican View

by

THOMAS J. TALLEY

SUMMARY

The "Agreed Statement on Eucharistic Doctrine" presently being studied by the Anglican and Roman Communions is less a contribution to liturgical convergence than it is an evidence of it. Roman Catholics and Episcopalians agree on the structure of the eucharistic liturgy and now use common versions of a great many liturgical texts. Is a common eucharistic prayer possible at this time? Will Episcopalians and Roman Catholics in the United States become one rite? Right now to help in our coming to a mutual understanding of ministry we need English texts which would for both Episcopalians and Roman Catholics employ the term "presbyter" to designate the second order of ministry and the term "priest" for that rich theological concept which we understand, with varying nuances, of Christ, of the episcopate, of the prebyterate, and of the Church herself. Roman Catholics and Episcopalians must maintain liaison and cooperation between the agencies of liturgical responsibility in their two churches.

I had the opportunity a few days ago to engage in conversation a brilliant young black theologian, and found myself struck by his insistence that one cannot do black theology if one comes to that enterprise armed with a tool box full of concepts developed in Western European theological discourse. Rather, he said, one must begin with the black American religious experience as fundamental datum, or even as that which black theology seeks to articulate in terms of the Gospel. Having already begun at that time to draft this statement, I was struck by the similarity of the problem he described and that which I was myself facing. For one does not approach the discussion of the liturgy or attempt to analyze liturgical development in terms of theological presuppositions or with theological concepts developed in a very different climate than that of the liturgy. The liturgical experience of the Church has, in the sacramental area, a certain primacy; sacramental theology, i.e., is theological reflection upon that tradition. Such questions as the definition of a sacrament or the number of them, or the nature of sacrifice or priesthood, do not have their answers independent of the liturgy and do not, therefore, serve well as points of departure. While one of the fruits of a serious examination of the liturgical tradition might well be to give answer to some of these questions, others might at that point and from that perspective seem less important questions or even disappear from the discussion.

To assess and appreciate the liturgical convergence of our Churches, therefore, we will do well to prescind from such questions and allow the liturgical phenomena to pose their own questions, to manifest their own developmental dynamic, and to offer their own promise. As perhaps the most powerful sentence in the *Constitution on the Sacred Liturgy* put it, "the liturgy is the summit toward which the activity of the Church is directed; at the same time it is the fountain from which all her power flows. For the goal of apostolic works is that all who are made sons of God by faith and baptism should come together to praise God in the midst of His Church, to take part in her sacrifice, and to eat the Lord's supper."[1]

In such a context we may say that the doctrinal accord on the eucharist reached by the Anglican/Roman Catholic International Commission in September 1971, while an achievement which deserves our most profound gratitude, and a step forward in our ecumenical relations of the most profound significance, is yet less a contribution to our liturgical convergence than it is an evidence of it. The liturgical reforms which have been at work in Anglicanism since the 18th century and have been particularly evident among Roman Catholics since Pius X have received renewed impetus in our present century through the recovery of early liturgical documents which have served to provide a primitive model against which we have been able to have a clearer understanding of our separate traditions and set our developments upon a common course.

Today, not only among Roman Catholics and Anglicans but from other quarters as well, we see the emergence of eucharistic liturgies which manifest the same fundamental and traditional structure: proclamation of the Word in scripture and preaching, common prayer in intercession, and the great eucharistic prayer which weaves over the gifts the themes of thanksgiving for all God's mighty actions, memorial of the mightiest of them all, and oblation of the gifts and of ourselves as the very substance of that memorial, to issue in the communion banquet where we are united with him who offered and offers himself, then and now, in that unique sacrifice in which we have been called and made to share. While our

69

eucharistic liturgies still show rich variety in detail, this variety is seldom today so overstated as to obscure that common tradition. If such a structural recovery seems a meager accomplishment, we should recall the situation of but a decade ago when the structural lacks and confusions of our liturgies reinforced at every point the lingering suspicions that we were up to different things, and probably with different Lords.

Beyond this emergence of a consensus regarding the structure of the eucharistic liturgy, a great many English speaking Christians now use common versions of a great many liturgical texts, a development whose theological import might not seem too great, but which strengthens that sense of cultural community which contributes to the dynamic of cultic convergence. Following an initiative taken by liturgists of the Missouri Synod of the Lutheran Church in this country, there was formed in 1967 a Consultation on Common Texts which became an international group two years later in consequence of an invitation extended by the International Committee on English in the Liturgy. The work of this International Consultation on English Texts has revealed the ecumenical force of a common culture. Such new expressions for traditional ideas are not easily accepted, but the patina of use forms rather quickly and the despised novelty will shortly inform still further the celebration which moves us to unity. That such common texts should have been sought at all reveals a deeper level of the process of vernacularization. For this process, whether it moves from Elizabethan English or from early medieval Latin, is not simply a matter of being understood. Vernacularization, rather, moves the tradition into contemporary culture, into that culture which we share in all our living, and so reveals itself as demanding a common expression of the meeting of our common culture and the one Gospel.

While the common texts presently in experimental use include the eucharistic dialogue and the sanctus, it is interesting that among the several eucharistic prayers in trial use among Episcopalians and the four anaphoras of the present Roman rite, there is still no one prayer which is the same for both churches, although the prayer of the second of the Episcopalian liturgies now in trial use and the second eucharistic prayer of the Roman rite are both derived, each in its own way, from a single source, the anaphora of the *Apostolic Tradition* of Hippolytus. It would seem an altogether laudable expression of the accord in eucharistic doctrine recently arrived at for Anglicans and Roman Catholics to undertake the approval of a eucharistic prayer which could be used by both, perhaps a common version of the Hippolytan prayer of which we both have versions at present (albeit versions which vary considerably in structure). This would be for both churches but one text among several and so would not represent a return to the rigidity of a single canon against which liturgical development in the past several years has demonstrated some reaction.

In candor, it should be recognized that such an undertaking would be extremely and perhaps prohibitively difficult to accomplish, given the many levels of liturgical authority that would be involved. Yet this difficulty itself raises the further interesting question of the degree of ritual uniformity which is to be expected in the future, given the deeper effect of vernacularization mentioned above. This question was raised already in sections 37-40 of the *Constitution on the Sacred Liturgy*, and certainly

71

the basic principle involved, that of ritual diversity, is one which has long been accepted.

Last year, it seemed to many that Pope Paul VI was making informal reference to the possibility of uniate status for Anglicans. Such a possibility seemed to many a pregnant one at the time of the Malines conversations in the last century, and it would indeed have been at least formally possible. The Roman rite at that time was the still highly fixed rite of Pius V, universally celebrated in Latin; the Anglican rite under question was that of the *Book of Common Prayer* of 1662, a liturgy which was vastly different from the Roman not only in language, but in content and structure. However, given the liturgical development of recent years, it is difficult now to see the exact meaning of the concept of Roman Catholics of the Anglican rite. On the one hand, there is no single American liturgy. Since 1634[2] the principle has been established among Anglicans that each national church should regulate its liturgical life, and each has indeed done so. Until recently these various national rites have still been clearly related to the English books, being largely rearrangements or modest emendations of the 1662 Prayer Book, usually aiming to bring it closer to the model of the first book of 1549. In the present ferment, however, the reforms are much more broadly based and the new generation of liturgical forms bears little textual relation to one another while all are more closely related to the commonly accepted traditional structure referred to above than was true of any at the opening of the century.

On the other hand, the great flexibility in the Roman rite today — completely free prayers of intercession, alternative forms of penitential action and four different anaphoras, all accommodated in various ways to local circumstances and translated into many different tongues, with the many subtle changes which accompany any translation — all this leads one to question the extent of uniformity in the Roman rite. Is there a single Roman rite today? There is, of course; but that would seem to be more a jurisdictional than a liturgical reality, in the strict sense. In point of fact, are we not moving to a time when the basis of liturgical unity is conformity to the central tradition rather than rubrical legislation — and this within the flexibility of the liturgical law itself? Such would certainly seem to be the case.

In such a circumstance, the impact of local culture is much heavier than would have been true with more rigidly determinative rubrical prescriptions. Thus, while it is difficult to see a single, unified Anglican rite which is so different from a single, unified Roman rite so as to make it possible for us to speak of uniate relations, it does seem that one might soon begin to speak of something like "uniate status" for American Roman Catholics, i.e., Roman Catholics of the American Rite. Something of the sort seems to be foreseen by the Constitution itself: "In virtue of power conceded by the law, the regulation of the liturgy within certain defined limits belongs also to various kinds of competent territorial bodies of bishops legitimately established."[3] While liturgical development has moved a long way since the promulgation of the Constitution, the liturgical prerogatives of the local episcopal conferences are still clearly circumscribed. Still, within that circumscription, it would behoove us to be mindful of the extent and value of our liturgical convergence and to seek to deepen it, for the community of our cultic life within our common culture

73

is already pledge and foretaste of the communion we seek. That communion itself will be the most powerful builder of our unity, to whatever extent we find it necessary to treat it as sign of a unity already realized. We cannot dissociate the elements of sign and causality in the sacramental life of the Church, but if the anomaly of disunity in the Body keeps us from communion for the present, we may yet be sure that the community of our liturgical experience of the Mystery of Christ is moving us and will continue to move us toward the unity to which that experience itself calls us.

Our liturgical convergence is a significant ecumenical force not only in the cultic/cultural terms in which we have been speaking; it should be important also for theological method where the sacraments are concerned. Yet just here we have a liturgical problem.

The recent ARC statement on *Doctrinal Agreement and Christian Unity* warns us of the problem of contextual transfer: "It should be recognized that past doctrinal utterances were made in definite cultural situations that are not our own, and hence that they reflect the presuppositions, terminology, and concerns of their times."[4] This observation seems particularly appropriate in relation to what seems likely to be the next area in which our ecumenical dialogue will seek consensus, the doctrine of the ministry. The concept of "sacrificing priesthood" so evident in earlier discussion of the ministry emerged in a theological climate which was not called upon to take account of the scriptural notion of the sacerdotality of the Church in quite the same way or to the same degree that we are today, and the establishment of balance has not been easy for either Roman Catholics or Anglicans. For both, "priesthood" has become a term suffused with values which are important from many standpoints, including the theological, but at the same time the term has become diffuse and imprecise because it contains two quite different concepts which cannot be so confused in the classical languages. In ancient languages the words designating that religious functionary whose role it was to offer sacrifice were utterly distinct from words designating the members of the ruling body of the community. In Hebrew the former was *kohen*, the latter *zaqen*; in Greek the former was *hiereus*, the latter *presbyteros*; in Latin the former was *sacerdos*, the latter *presbyter* (borrowed from the Greek; although *senior* is not unknown). The New Testament applies sacerdotal terminology only to Christ (in the Epistle to the Hebrews) and to the Church (in I Peter and the Apocalypse), but by the end of the second century this terminology was being extended to the liturgical president. In the earlier sources this is most explicitly the bishop, though this sacerdotal reference was being extended to the presbyters shortly after and is established by the middle of the third century, the linguistic usage expanding as did the frequency of presbyteral presidency at the eucharist. By the 11th century the presbyter was so much the normal president at the eucharist that his order was treated and spoken of as the normal locus of *sacerdotium*. When, then, the vernaculars became the vehicles of theological and liturgical discourse in the 16th century, the two concepts were conflated in vernacularized forms of the Latin *presbyter*: *priester*, *prestre*, priest. This term has since then been used to render both *presbyter* and *sacerdos* with a resultant confusion which makes the vernacular liturgical documents more a symptom of the problem than the source of its solution.

For this reason, it would seem to be a matter of considerable importance for our new vernacular texts to re-
establish the distinction between these two before they
become too hallowed by usage. In the new Episcopalian
ordination rites currently in trial use the most common
term for a minister of the second order is "priest," although "presbyter" is used when reference is made to
the presbyteral college as a group. The International
Committee on English in the Liturgy, rather more
significantly, follows the Latin distinction at several sensitive points, most notably in that portion of the ordination prayer designated by Pope Pius XII as the sacramental form of the ordination: [5]

> We ask you, all-powerful Father, give these serv-
> ants of yours the dignity of the presbyterate. Re-
> new the Spirit of holiness within them. By your
> divine gift may they attain the second order in
> the hierarchy (*secundi meriti munus obtineant*)
> and exemplify right conduct in their lives.
>
> *(The Ordination of Priests, 22)*

Both our churches, therefore, employ both terms, yet
both fail thus far to use these consistently to express the
distinction of the tradition which is carefully preserved
in the Latin texts. This would be difficult for Anglicans,
since four centuries of use and original materials which
have no Latin counterpart have to a great extent ob-
scured the distinction. Yet a reconstruction would in
most cases be possible. It would be, it seems, a considerable help in our coming to a mutual understanding of
the views of ministry manifested in our new rites of
ordination if we could have, at least for study, English
texts which would, for both our rites, consistently employ the term "presbyter" to designate the second order

of ministry and all that pertains specifically to it, and the term "priest" for that rich theological concept which we understand, with varying nuances, of Christ, of the episcopate, of the presbyterate, and of the Church herself. Until we can do something of this sort, the problem of "contextual transfer" which was so properly pointed out in the ARC statement cited above threatens to muddy the liturgical springs of the Church's traditional wisdom.

We should have no fear that such clarification of the issue would weaken the evidence of our liturgical convergence in the area of holy orders and so render more difficult that attainment of doctrinal consensus which is a proximate goal of our dialogue. Indeed, one of the more notable evidences of our liturgical convergence is precisely in this area of ordination, viz., the adoption by both the Episcopal Church (for trial use) and the Roman Pontifical of the ordination prayer for a bishop from the *Apostolic Tradition* of Hippolytus, even though this meant for Anglicans moving away from the habit of ordination by declarative formula which we inherited from the common medieval view, and for Roman Catholics giving up a prayer hallowed by constant use for a millenium and a half. The common use of this third century form for the ordination of a bishop (in different translations but clearly parallel texts) is perhaps the clearest evidence of the convergence of our living traditions in this particularly sensitive area.

Such seem to be, from the standpoint of a liturgiologist, a few of the more significant evidences of our movement toward unity in the cultic area, some of the ways in which that movement might be strengthened, and the importance which we should attach to both. We may hope, finally, that as ancillary to the dedicated theological work of ARC and ARCIC the closest attention will be paid to the maintenance of liaison and cooperation between the agencies of liturgical responsibility in our two churches. In yet other areas, such as rites of initiation, we have uniquely common problems and a common tradition troubled at present by considerable ferment and a common need for clarification. It would be a regrettable dereliction if we should find ourselves diverging from one another through mere inattention, and this in an area which has never been a problem between us.

History shows us with painful regularity that cultic community is no safeguard against schism. But it shows us just as plainly that the dissolution of communion brings cultic divergence. Such liturgical convergence as we presently enjoy is more unprecedented, and must be received as manifestation of the ecclesial and liturgical presence and dynamically creative will of him, the High Priest of our profession, who offered the sacrifice of his life in the prayer, "Father, I will that they be one."

A Roman Catholic View

by

JOHN GALLEN, S.J.

SUMMARY

Both in the celebration of liturgy and the theological science of liturgy the Churches are experiencing a growing convergence of attitude and practice. The convergence is occurring on the very meaning of liturgy itself. Because of this convergence, contemporary man's need to overcome his experience of alienation can be met by the Church's rich and ancient tradition of the liturgy of reconciliation. In this tradition the principal liturgy of reconciliation is the Eucharist. Eucharist is *the* sacrament of forgiveness. The Eucharist, therefore, should be the model for reforming and developing liturgies of penance and reconciliation.

The task of liturgical reform which the churches have undertaken during recent years has raised a series of questions about the nature of liturgy as ritual action. This renewal of interest in liturgy and in liturgical reform and development has, at the same time, raised questions about the proper academic approach to worship as a theological enterprise. In both of these areas, the celebration of liturgy and the theological science of liturgy, we are able to detect in the churches a growing convergence of attitude and practice.

Positively speaking, the renewed interest in the study of the interrelationship between man's symbol-making ritual activity and the contemporary forms of religious life which stand behind such activity not only puts the churches more solidly in contact with the deeply traditional understanding of worship as *sacramentum fidei*; it also provides the outlines of a theological methodology which, while it places high value on the importance of the history of the liturgy, is only content when a large percentage of its data are the elements of contemporary religious man's life. Thus, we begin to experience the beginnings of both practical and theological convergence among the churches in worship.

With regard to practice, when the reformed liturgies now in the process of being instituted by the churches are examined, it is clear that scholarship which deals with a common Tradition has been creating liturgies which represent the heart and center of that Tradition, and therefore has been creating liturgies which, quite similar in content and structure, are a sign of our convergence in one common Tradition. The liturgies of Eucharist are a clear example (note especially those of Anglican, Lutheran and Roman backgrounds). With regard to the theological science of liturgy, everyone is aware that, negatively speaking, a sheerly historicist approach to worship does not contribute those insights concerning the contemporary religious experience of men in a particular cultural-historical moment of time which are able to raise the interest of scholars and of believers-at-prayer in any significant way beyond the level of antiquarianism.

A common view of the nature of liturgy is already an emerging reality. Because of our study of the Tradition, we already possess together an increasingly mature appreciation of Eucharist and, in particular, of Eucharist as the primary sacrament of reconciliation. With Eucharist as model, we may now go on to develop other appropriate liturgies of reconciliation for the prayer of men in our time.

Liturgy is *sacramentum fidei.* To make use of this formula is in reality, of course, another way of affirming the equally venerable adage, *lex orandi est lex credendi,* that is, that the shape of the community's prayer mirrors the shape of its life-in-faith.

The immediately pressing question becomes, in this context, a question about the community's life-in-faith. Where the community finds itself at one moment or other of history, how the community experiences the presence of the Holy One, the form and the dimensions of the self-disclosure which the God of Mystery makes of himself — all of this is what the community brings to its prayer together. All of this is what the community sacramentalizes in its prayer together. The community's faith-experience, the *lex credendi*, is ritualized, is spelled out in the action of the community's *lex orandi*, its prayer in common. The problem of liturgy is seen to be quite exactly the problem of God. The liturgical question needs to be formulated as a revelation-question.

Liturgy is not a free-floating "religious" event, a "sacred" moment which has escaped the alien, destructive and enervating pollution that resides in the air and atmosphere of day-to-day experience. It is not a moment of absolute truth which soars independently secure from the compromising half-truths and tentative gropings of daily life. It is not a *given* in a world of *to-be-founds*. We can never say that liturgy is the truth in our lives together. Liturgy can never be for us, as we affirm it to be, the celebration of the Paschal Mystery unless we are already plunged, each moment together, into the death and rising of Jesus.

This view of liturgical worship, which places emphasis upon the community prayer-experience as both the *reflection of* and the *deepening of* the ways in which the community has already begun to experience the Lord's presence, represents a considerable advance in the churches' approach. It is an advance because it refuses to opt for *either* LITURGY-AS-EXPRESSION *or* LITURGY-AS-CAUSE of religious experience in the community. It insists on taking *both* dimensions of liturgical prayer *together*. When the implications of this more realistic and thoroughly traditional approach to liturgy are applied to concrete situations of community significance, their import emerges with convincing clarity.

With regard to the question of the validation of one's

ministry in the community, for example, if one regards liturgy as an experience of community prayer in which the priesthood, which has already been the work of God's Spirit in an individual, is celebrated and summoned to its fullness, then it is not possible to think that ministry is created in the liturgy of ordination. It begins with what we classically describe as "election," and is developed and elaborated through many experiences and grace-filled years as one moves along the way of pilgrimage with the Lord, being finally brought to its flowering and completion in the community prayer of ordination. When believers and believer-theologians take this approach to liturgy, they repudiate both a gnostic conception of religion as an exclusively interior and esoteric experience, as well as the rather magical view which suggests that liturgies create realities *ex nihilo*, with never a consideration given to the already-existing religious involvement of an individual or community. The truth is that worship is neither gnostic nor magical. It is *celebratory*. It celebrates an already-existing reality and, in this festivity, enlarges, under the power of God's Spirit, the reality that is God's work in us.

One of the areas of liturgical prayer which has begun to receive a new and deserved attention is the liturgy of reconciliation. The community prayer of reconciliation deserves the attention that we give it today because of contemporary man's felt need to overcome his experience of alienation and estrangement which has so often been generated by the emergence of the new world-consciousness that has crystallized in our age. Man undergoes today an experience of sinfulness and guilt which participates so fully in this sensation of alienation that it has readily quickened a desire for union and reconciliation within a community of brothers and sisters who glory in the abundance of one life poured out upon them by the one Lord of history.

The task before us then is to help in fostering this admirable and holy quest for reconciliation by offering and making available ritual actions in which men of our time may pray together and so come to more and more complete union of hearts and lives. As we do so, it is important to note that the horizons of this task go well beyond the situation of the Anglican and Roman Churches and provide the context in which these churches approach their work. Happily, though, we do not come to the task entirely without resources.

The first element of resource is a primary affirmation of the Church's Tradition that *Eucharist* is the privileged celebration of reconciliation in the Christian community. The background of this affirmation, of course, is derived from the New Testament data concerning Jesus' ministry of table-fellowship. We refer here quite directly to the way in which Jesus chose to ritualize his preaching concerning the Kingdom of God and the offer of universal reconciliation and salvation for all men without exception. This ministry of table-fellowship which unfolded in the three stages of (1) his public life, (2) the Last Supper and (3) the risen appearances proclaimed that all men were invited to share in the experience of the presence of the Holy One and thus to experience the Kingdom. The ritual sign and symbol of this invitation and experience was the shared table. As Paul himself was to theologize, all who shared in the one bread shared in the one life of God. So characteristic of Jesus in the New Testament was this ministry of table-fellowship that finally it was the way to recognize him, to know his presence *in fractione panis*, in the breaking of the bread.

This same ministry of table-fellowship was handed over by Jesus to the primitive community. Their Eucharist, their shared table, was the Eucharist of Jesus, the continued proclamation of Kingdom: the Holy One offers universal reconciliation, salvation for all. It is this same ministry which has been handed down to us, believers in the Lord Jesus and his Word. Our Eucharistic celebration announces the same offer of reconciliation. Eucharist, as the paschal celebration of the Christian community, in announcing the death and rising of Jesus, announces the new Passover from death to life in the Kingdom. The Eucharist is thus the primary and privileged celebration of our reconciliation.

It is not possible to maintain that this explicit interrelationship between Eucharist and reconciliation has always been in the center of the conscious awareness of the Church. Nevertheless, as Jean-Marie Tillard has written:

> In the most realistic sense of the term, the Eucharist is the sacrament of forgiveness, because it is the sacramental presence and communication of the act which remits sins: as the remembrance of the expiation of the cross, it applies that expiation to those who celebrate the memorial by putting them in touch, through the bread and the cup of the meal, with the "once and for all" of the paschal event itself, and calls down on the whole world the infinite mercy of God, the Father of Jesus. Within the Church, it is properly speaking the location of redemption![1]

84

And Elmer Arndt writes on the same point:

> Participation in the supper is participation in the remission of sins won for us by Jesus' self-sacrifice . . . Because of Christ's atoning death, man is now placed in a new status before God; for God acting through Christ has dealt with sin and offered free forgiveness. Participation in the Lord's Supper is, for believers, appropriation of the divine forgiveness.[2]

As constant as this Tradition has been in the Church, both East and West, not much attention has been paid to it in recent years. As Tillard points out, "It seems that, at least for several centuries, the Latin Church has not been very much interested in the dimension of 'pardon' that belongs to the eucharistic mystery. As a result, there has been perhaps an exaggerated amount of attention given to sacramental penance, to the detriment of a more balanced view of the whole sacramental economy of forgiveness."[3]

The first part of our task, therefore, is to recover and teach this important and central element of the Church's Tradition regarding liturgical celebration of reconciliation and forgiveness. In particular, new Eucharistic Prayers need to be composed which bring out pointedly the reconciliation-dimensions of the Supper to which we are invited. The *epiclesis* of this great Prayer of Blessing should elaborate the invocation in such a way that clear reference to the Spirit's work of purifying, transforming, unifying and bringing reconciliation to the hearts of men would emerge.

The second element for consideration in our project of reforming and developing liturgies of penance and reconciliation is the need to fashion communal celebrations of penance for use by the community outside of Eucharist. It is true that there already has been extensive experimentation with several forms of this type of liturgy, but I do not believe that it is possible to say that they have been altogether successful. One important reason for their lack of success is, in my judgment, that they are not sufficiently inspired by what the Tradition can offer them. The attempt has often been made in the Roman Church, for example, to focus the center of such a communal service on an "absolution" given in general to the community. While the intended purpose of this communal absolution was indeed admirable, hoping to place emphasis on the community dimensions of sinfulness and forgiveness, the form of rituals thus far employed leaves, I would suggest, something to be desired. Rather than making use of a truncated form of the Prayer of Blessing (which was the origin of the absolution formula employed as the practice of private auricular confession became widespread), this communal liturgy of penance should be made to rest its entire weight upon the Prayer of Blessing given in its fullness. The structure and content of this prayer, derived from the Jewish tradition of *berakah*, should proclaim the presence of the Holy One, praise the Lord for the ways in which he has touched us with his presence, invoke his Spirit of loving forgiveness, union and reconciliation, and end in doxology.

While Scripture readings and homily might well precede the Blessing Prayer, and while there is room to elaborate ritual gesture as a sign of reconciliation, the Blessing Prayer itself should be the heart and center of a new communal liturgy of penance.

The third and final element in the process of reform is a renewal of what has been called "private auricular confession." To do so, one must have immediate recourse to the history and meaning of this form of prayer. Its origin in monasticism of both East and West was, of course, as a form of the mutual discernment of spirits. Its original situation was one in which a Christian consulted with his spiritual Father, seeking to learn the motions of the Spirit within himself, to see more clearly the ways to grow in the Life of the Spirit and to know the causes and reasons for his infidelities.

When the rich possibilities of this kind of mutual prayer are taken into account, one must conclude that it does not appear helpful to eliminate private auricular confession. What is to be eliminated are the abusive forms of its practice. Tradition helps us again on this point. We must recover and be inspired by the ancient Tradition of mutual discernment and prayer for forgiveness which was such a rich form of the penitential ritual. When we have done so, we will again be able to speak with our people, the People of God, about "confession" in a way that responds to their developing consciousness of sin, guilt and forgiveness.

IV

MINISTRY AND ORDERS

The Ministry in the
New Testament

by
REGINALD H. FULLER

SUMMARY

Modern biblical scholarship has called into question the presuppositions of traditional Anglican apologetic for episcopacy.
Acts and the *Pastoral Epistles* are evidence not for Paul, whose
Churches had purely charismatic ministries, but witness to the
"early catholic" development of an ordered ministry, a development not completed until after the New Testament period.
Episcopacy (and also the recognition of the priestly character
of the ministry) must now be justified in terms of legitimate
development.

Modern critical scholarship recognizes that the New
Testament is a pluralistic book. The various authors do
not speak with a single voice on any topic, save on their
central witness to Jesus Christ as the saving act of God.
Besides the variety of individual authors, there are three
main strata in the New Testament writings: the Jesus
tradition, the apostolic age, and — as modern critical
scholarship is making increasingly clear (pseudonymity
and later dating) — the subapostolic age. The Jesus tradition does not directly concern us for the history of the
ministry in the New Testament period, but the other

two strata do. The apostolic age is represented by the primitive kerygmatic materials in Acts and Paul, by the Pauline homologoumena (1 Thessalonians, Galatians, 1 and 2 Corinthians, Philippians, Philemon, Romans), by the Palestinian and Hellenistic modifications and additions to the Jesus tradition in the oral stage prior to the written Gospels, and — right at the fringe of the apostolic age — by the Gospel of Mark. The subapostolic age (which I date roughly from 70 to 125) is represented in the New Testament by the Pauline antilegomena (Colossians, Ephesians, Hebrews, and the catholic epistles), by the Evangelists' redaction in Matthew and Luke, and by the compositional elements in the Johannine literature.

The Earliest Community

The Jerusalem church came into being on the foundation of Peter and the Twelve; the church spread beyond Jerusalem prior to Paul through the witness of "all the *apostoloi*" (1 Corinthians 15:7). Their precise relation to the Twelve, whether identical, overlapping or distinct, is unclear. In my view they are overlapping. It was Paul's understanding of his apostolic task that he should found churches. Some communities no doubt came into existence without direct apostolic foundation (e.g., the Hellenistic communities founded after Stephen's martyrdom, and the Roman community before the expulsion of the Jews in 48). Such foundations may be regarded as extensions of the missions of the apostles. The people who founded them were dependent on the apostles for the gospel, which focussed on Jesus Christ as the eschatological act of God to which the Twelve and all the apostles were accredited witnesses. Later on, apostles show up at churches which were founded as extensions of their mission (e.g., Peter, Barnabas, and Paul at Antioch; Paul and — probably — Peter at Rome). Paul as an apostle continued to exercise oversight over the churches he founded by visits and correspondence.

The government and ongoing ministry in the local communities during the apostolic age presents a complex and opaque picture. At Jerusalem, James came to exercise a quasi-monarchical authority over a "sanhedrin" of elders on the Jewish model, and no doubt this sanhedrin pattern was copied in other communities of the Jewish mission (cf. James 5:14). But in the period covered by Acts the functions of this "sanhedrin" seem to have been governmental and administrative. How the ministry of word and sacrament was performed in the Palestinian communities at this period is unclear. But if the indirect hints of the special Matthean material can be taken as evidence, it would have been performed by prophets and teachers (Matthew 7:15; 23:8)). At Antioch, a mixed community, partly Jewish and partly Gentile, prophets and teachers evidently exercised both governmental and pastoral-liturgical functions (Acts 13:1-3), which appears to be old tradition being contrary to Luke's redactional presentation of ministries.

The Pauline Communities

In the Pauline churches charismatic ministries seem to have been the norm. The evidence about this is clearest in 1 Corinthians 12-14 which presents us with a welter of charismatics. Listed numerically in order of importance (1 Corinthians 12:28f) are apostles, prophets and teachers, whose functions seem to have been exercised in a more or less permanent basis and so have given names to the functionaries. It is surprising to find apostles in this list, since Paul normally uses the term for an accredited witness of the resurrection appointed for mission in a resurrection appearance. Here apostles are creations of the Spirit in the church. I believe Paul is here using the word in a different sense. These apostles are wandering missionaries, such as appeared in the Pauline churches, often as false apostles (2 Corinthians). They are probably a development from Antioch and the Hellenistic missionaries after Stephen.[1] The fact that they were so often false apostles led to their eventual demise, though there is evidence for their continued existence in Revelation and Didache. The prophets and teachers we have already noticed at Antioch, and they appear again here (cf. Romans 12:6-7). As the discussion in 1 Corinthians 12-14 indicates, prophets were responsible for the ministry of the word and liturgical leadership, including the recitation of the eucharistic prayer (1 Corinthians 14:16; Paul finds this being done in tongues at Corinth, but would prefer it to be done by intelligible prophecy). Teachers would be responsible for handing on catechetical tradition (cf. Romans 6:17). At Corinth the governmental functions (helps, governments) were on a different level. This in indicated by two facts: first, they are not enumerated "first," "second" and "third" as the primary charismata, and second, they are designated as charismata, not by the personal functionaries who exercise them. This suggests that such functions were performed on an *ad hoc* basis. At Philippi things were different. There Paul addresses "bishops and deacons." Evidently in this community, unlike Corinth, governmental and administrative functions hardened into quasi-permanent offices.[2] In the other Pauline communities we hear of people who exercised leadership of various kinds. We would probably not be wrong in inferring from the highly deliberate and systematic character of the list in 1 Corinthians 12, that these, like the functionaries at Philippi, were charismatics. This is contrary to the traditional view as enunciated e.g., by H. J. Carpenter, the former Bishop of Oxford, who argued[3] that 1 Corinthians 12 merely described the variety of functions in the one body, and does not enumerate ecclesiastical offices. The deliberately systematic character of the charismatic list shows otherwise. Other references to ministry in the Pauline homologoumena must be understood in the light of that list, not vice versa.

Ordination in the Apostolic Age

The homologoumena never mention ordination. The inference that it was practiced in the Pauline churches rests upon Acts 14 and 20 and the Pastorals, that is, evidence which according to modern critical opinion comes from the subapostolic age, not from the Pauline period. It would seem that the charismata welled up as it were spontaneously in the communities (cf. Stephen as in 1 Corinthians 16:15). Such a view was rejected by conservative Anglican apologetic, but I am glad that it finds support from that critical though Catholic-minded Episcopalian scholar, Burton Scott Easton.[4]

On the other hand it is reasonable to suppose that, in the Palestinian communities, the elders would have been ordained by the laying on of hands, since it was already Jewish practice,[5] though this is admittedly an argument from silence. However, it must be remembered that these elders performed governmental, not pastoral-liturgical, functions. There, too, the prophets and teachers would presumably have been charismatic, but not ordained. At the same time, it must also be remembered that strictly pastoral-liturgical functions, at least in the Pauline communities, which is all we know about, were under the supervision and control of the apostles.

The Subapostolic Period

In turning to the ministry during the subapostolic age, we find that the evidence falls into two main groups, an earlier and a later. The earlier group consists of Ephesians, Hebrews, 1 Peter 1-4:11; the later group of 1 Peter 4:12-end, Acts and Pastorals.

The Earlier Subapostolic Writings

We have already noted a certain hardening of ecclesiastical office in the bishops and deacons of Philippians 1:1 towards the end of the Pauline period. This tendency is further mirrored in an early deutero-Pauline charismatic list, namely Ephesians 4:11-16, which is clearly modeled on the Pauline lists (1 Corinthians 12:28, Romans 12:6f). It is similarly systematic, featuring the preeminent charismata by connecting particles, *men . . . de . . . de*. But there are changes. The charismata are now the gifts of the ascended Christ, not of the Spirit in the Church. There is a change in the items in the list. Apostles are still first, and prophets second, but the third place is taken by evangelists, while what was originally the third item, the teachers, is now placed fourth and expanded to include "shepherds." I take it though that pastors and teachers refer to a single office, for they are included within a common article. Ephesians, an "early catholic" writing, looks back on the apostles and prophets as belonging to the now post-apostolic age. The

93

"evangelists" will be immediate successors of the apostles, people like the actual authors of the deutero-Pauline letters and of the catholic epistles, as opposed to the apostolic names which they bear. These are the group whom Bishop Gore designated as "apostolic men." They possess authority over groups of churches, and can address these churches over the heads of their local leadership, and over the local leaders themselves. The shepherds and teachers form the local leadership. The community addressed in this letter has brought together the originally separate functions for teaching and government. This is the germ of the *presbuteroi*⁶ as they appear later in Acts and Pastorals. Meanwhile, the minor charismata have disappeared from the picture entirely.

There is still nothing about ordination in Ephesians: the ministries are still freely charismatic, though it is now the ascended Christ who appoints them. This prepares the way for the emergence of ordination for the presbyter-bishops as we shall see in the later group of subapostolic writings.

Hebrews, though its evidence is scanty, belongs to roughly the same stage of development as Ephesians, which is not surprising since it has some definite relation with the deutero-Pauline literature. Hebrews 13:17 refers to the "leaders" (*hegoumenoi*). Here a personal description of a church office is intended. There are traces of this term applied similarly to a church office in Luke 22:26, the remodelling of a Jesus saying in the light of developing church order.⁷ They appear in early catholic writings outside the New Testament (1 Clement, Hermas). All the emphasis in Hebrews is on the proper relation of the leaders to the "saints" (*Hagioi*, the ordinary members of the community).⁸ Their functions include, like the pastor-teachers of Ephesians, both ministry of the word (13:37) and governmental-pastoral duties (vs. 17), i.e., the care of souls. This church office the original founders also shared (cf. fellow-elder Peter in 1 Peter 5:1). This suggests some incipient notion of apostolic succession. Nothing is said in Hebrews of their charismatic status. Buchsel comments: "Whether the leaders are chosen by the community or appointed by their predecessors, whether they are charismatics or how they are related to the charismatics . . . remains obscure. Their authority is stressed, but it resides not in their persons but in their function: they must give account for their care of souls."[9] On the other hand, Otto Michel in his commentary on Hebrews (*ad loc*) observes that the way in which their authority rests upon the word they proclaim suggests that they may still have been free charismatics, though not of the fanatic type. In them the Spirit, as Paul would insist, is subject to the criterion of the Word. In my opinion, the leaders of Hebrews represent a transition from the free charismatic to institutional office.

1 Peter 4:11 comes from the first part of the letter, which was probably a baptismal homily. It follows a common pattern in concluding an eschatological exhortation, together with an admonition to the local ministry. This is still fully charismatic (vs. 10: "as *each one* has received the *charisma*"). The charismata are shared by all members of the body. Nevertheless, the only charismata about which the writer gives specific injunctions are the ministry of the word and *diakonia*. The charismata are clearly hardening into a twofold institutional ministry of the word and of *diakonia*. We are thus in a transition stage between the Pauline multiplicity of

charismata, and a two-fold local ministry of presbyter-bishops and deacons.

The Later Subapostolic Writings of the New Testament

It is instructive to compare the passage from 1 Peter, which we have just examined, with a passage from the later part of the letter, which serves to adapt the baptismal homily as an epistle. The passage in question (1 Peter 5:1-4) speaks of *presbuteroi* (elders). But it does so in a context of exhortations to older and younger members of the church. This shows the patriarchal origin of the term *presbuteroi*. The sanhedrins in the Palestinian Christian communities had doubtless been patriarchal, as in the synagogue. But now, as the injunction to shepherd the flock in vs. 2 shows, the originally patriarchally conceived presbyters are assuming pastoral functions. In other words, the presbyterate has become a ministerial office. This takes us a little further than Ephesians 4, where there were teachers and shepherds, for the latter have now been fully institutionalized as *presbuteroi*. Correspondingly, the local congregation over which they have charge is called a "flock" (vs. 3), and significantly the exalted Christ is called the *archipoimen*, the chief Shepherd.[10] The shepherds are under-shepherds of Christ, agents through whom his shepherding is made visibly and effectively present in the community. Such a development of thinking would seem to imply a permanent, institutionalized type of ministry.

Were these officers ordained? Perhaps the exhortation that they should perform their office "not under constraint, but willingly" (vs. 2) suggests this. Being appointed by ordination, they might have regarded themselves as conscripted into service! "Not for sordid financial gain" (vs. 2) suggests that they were paid officers too (cf. Pastoral epistles). "Not lording it over the flock" (vs. 3) suggests that the presbyters exercised disciplinary functions. Nothing is said about the ministry of the word, but perhaps the author who added the latter part intended the reader to apply what the earlier part, the baptismal homily, had said (1 Peter 4:11) about the charismata to this now institutionalized ministry.

Finally, note that the elders enjoy a special relation to the apostle under whose aegis this letter is written, for Peter is called a fellow-presbyter (5:1). This suggests two points. First, the pseudonymous author of the epistolary part, writing in Peter's name, claims collegiality with the local ministry, he himself being an "apostolic man" type, like the evangelists and the pseudonymous author of Ephesians. Second, the institutionalized ministry of the subapostolic generation claims a real continuity of function with the apostle, and hence, by implication, some kind of succession in office.

The second rather later writing to which we turn is Acts. The relevant passages are Acts 14:22 and 20:17-18. Unlike the older scholarship, contemporary scholarship[11] regards these passages, not as historical, but as redactional. That is, they reflect the ministerial set-up with which the author of Luke-Acts was familiar in the last decade of the first century. Acts 14:23 makes Paul and Barnabas ordain (*cheirotonesantes*)[12] presbyters in every city on the first missionary journey. Historically this is most improbable, for there is nothing to suggest this in the Pauline homologoumena. It is a commonly accepted methodological principle among critical New

Testament scholars that the homologoumena must be accepted as primary evidence for Paul, and Acts only where it is consistent with the authentic Pauline evidence.[13] But Acts 14:23 is excellent evidence for the subapostolic age. Here we have a local ministry consisting of a college of presbyters ordained in succession from the apostles. The author of Luke-Acts wants us, I think, to assume that this was regular Pauline practice. Hence in chapter 20 he can introduce elders from Ephesus who gather for Paul's farewell address. This address, which modern critical scholarship understands as a Lucan composition, is almost a compendium of subapostolic thinking on the ministry. To begin with, we note that in vs. 28 the elders are addressed as *episcopoi*, showing that at this period the two terms are synonymous. Secondly, we note that these presbyter-bishops are entrusted with the guardianship of the truth of the gospel in the period after the apostle's death, and this in face of the "wolves," false teachers (gnostics?) who will arise after the apostles' departure.

Here we have an important clue to the development of an institutionalized ministry. The free-for-all charismatic situation which prevailed in the Pauline churches is no longer acceptable in the church of the subapostolic age. Two new factors have emerged: 1) the demise of the original witnesses; 2) the threat of gnosticism and the need to preserve the truth of the gospel. Ordained ministry in succession is part (though let me emphasize only a part: there are other factors, the crystallization of the *paratheke*, i.e., the deposit of faith in credal formulae, and the gradual growth of the New Testament canon) of the attempt to subordinate the Spirit to the Word, which had been precisely Paul's concern in writing 1 Corinthians. It is part, I say, of the endeavor to maintain the apostolicity of the church in the period when the original apostolic witnesses are no longer around and to see that the ministry and government and pastoral care of the flock is still carried out in fidelity to that witness. Finally, let us note that the farewell address still recognizes the charismatic character of the ministry, even after it has become institutionalized. It is the Holy Spirit which makes men *episcopoi* (20:28), even though this now occurs in and through the human acts of laying on of hands and prayer. Strictly it is wrong, even though convenient, to contrast "charismatic" and institutional in speaking of the development of the ministry from the apostolic to the subapostolic age. The real contrast is between spontaneous and institutional.

The picture in the Pastoral epistles is very much the same. It is of course assumed with the majority of modern critical scholars that these letters are not by Paul, but by a later member of the Pauline school. We need not discuss the evidence in detail. The writer speaks of ministerial succession (2 Timothy 2:2). He pictures a local ministry consisting of presbyters (apparently also called bishops, but see below) and deacons. Their function is to read and proclaim the word of God, to guard the apostolic faith (*paratheke*, deposit), to administer discipline. Ordination is apparently practiced universally through the laying on of hands with prayer. The institutional character of this ministry is indicated by the fact that not only are the ministers ordained in this way, but the qualifications for their selection and arrangements for their payment are set out in detail. Here is a veritable church order.

There are of course certain residual problems. The first concerns the place of the "Timothy" and "Titus" in this scheme, and related with this the problem of the *episcopos*. Some have argued that, since the term *presbuteros* normally occurs in the plural and *episcopos* invariably in the singular, the two terms are no longer synonymous as in Acts, but that the single *episcopos* is already beginning to emerge.[14] Others hold, more plausibly, that this oscillation of number is due to the fact that the author is drawing upon a traditional code (*Bischofsspiegel*).[15] I think the latter is the more likely explanation for the change of number. If we are to see the germs of the monarchical episcopate (or more accurately, of the *monepiscopos*) anywhere in the past, I think we are to see it in the "Timothy" and the "Titus." It is these who have responsibility for the oversight of a plurality of churches. It is these who are responsible for the oversight and discipline of the local ministers. The "Timothy" and the "Titus" are symbols for the actual author of the Pastoral epistles, who is one of the authors who lie behind the apostolic pseudonyms used in all the literature of this period. They occupy a place midway between the apostles in the first period and the *monepiscopos* of the second century.

The ministerial functions spelled out in the Pastorals were written. It is to be noted, however, that there is no question in this period of connecting eucharistic presidency with succession. Succession is envisaged rather as the external means of handing on the apostolic tradition of faith.

Ordination, as the later New Testament writers understand it, does not necessarily mean that the charismata are the exclusive monopoly of the ordained. Even

2 Peter, for example, appeals frequently to a *consensus fidelium*. In the writings of which we are speaking, the intention is that the preeminent charismata, those which concern the ministry of word, should be exercised in the context of and under the control of the apostolic witness. As Edmund Schlink has put it as a Lutheran systematician:

> The relationship between Word and Spirit, between the historical uniqueness of God's salvation and the continuity of the saving Word of the Spirit (which is at the very basis of church life), finds its proper expression in the insistence on special commission. For the work of the Spirit is to stir the believer's memory; by this we mean that he is always referring back to the unique and historical saving act of Jesus Christ, and in doing this, he points back to the apostolic word, and actualizes this same salvation. Thus the Spirit and the Word are not contradictory, far from it, they belong together.[16]

The Priesthood

It is well-known that the New Testament studiously avoids using the term priest (*hiereus, sacerdos*) for the ministry in the church. It is confined to the Christ himself, and also used generally for the whole priestly body of the church. Two observations, however, can be made: in the subapostolic age, sacrificial language is beginning to be used of the eucharist (Hebrews 13:10 and 15). The language of 1 Peter 2:1-10, applied to the whole priestly body, while having a deliberately ethical slant, implies that the concrete focus of the priestly activity of the whole body is liturgical and cultic. "Showing forth the

101

praises of him who called us from darkness into his own marvelous light" is an apt description of the contents of the great eucharistic prayer. Moreover, Paul has already used priestly language of his own apostolic ministry of bringing Gentile converts into the *ecclesia* (Romans 15:15).

From a New Testament point of view, therefore, it would seem to be at once hazardous and justifiable to use the term "priest" of a Christian minister. It is hazardous because it can easily suggest that the Old Testament priesthood abolished by Christ is being revived, because it can obscure the scriptural doctrines of the finality of Christ's high-priesthood, or obscure the priesthood of the whole body of the church. It is justified because at the very lowest level the minister is as much a sharer in the priesthood of the whole body as any of the non-ministerial members of the body. And more than that, it is the minister who has the particular responsibility of articulating and expressing the priesthood of the whole body. In this sense, then, he must be a priest. But the New Testament would seem to justify a functional, rather than ontological concept of priesthood. And the word "priest" (except when it is equivalent to "presbyter," one of the ambiguities of the English and other modern European languages) ought to be used only when we are speaking in a functional context.

Does the pluralism of the New Testament mean that any kind of ministry is legitimate ("Everyone has won, and all shall have prizes"[17])? Or does it mean that the New Testament witnesses to a process that is as yet incomplete, that certain lines have been established which will eventually converge towards the stabilized institutions of the patristic church? The latter has been the position of Anglicanism, and it is reinforced by the modern critical study of the New Testament. Speaking of episcopacy, the Lambeth Bishops wrote in 1930:

The Episcopate occupies a position which is, in point of historical development, analogous to that of the Canon of Scripture and the creeds. In the first days there was no Canon of the New Testament Scripture, for the books afterwards included in it were still being written. For a time, different churches had different writings which they regarded as authoritative. The Canon was slowly formed and the acceptance of a single Canon throughout the Church took several generations. So, too, the Apostles' Creed is the result of a process of growth which we can in large measure trace. If the Episcopate, as we find it universally by the end of the second century, was the result of a like process of adaptation and growth, that would be no evidence that it lacked divine authority, but rather that the life of the Spirit within the Church had found it to be the most appropriate organ for the functions it discharged.[18]

We can only justify our institutions in terms of legitimate development. This applies to priesthood, episcopacy, and succession. Could it also, for Anglicans, legitimate the development of the primacy of the Bishop of Rome?

Roman Catholic Views on Ordained Ministry

by
JOHN LINNAN, C.S.V.

SUMMARY

Currently Roman Catholic theologians are trying to evaluate the ministry of other Christian communities by asking whether these communities are truly churches, for, if they are, it would seem that their ministry is also sacramental. What makes a Christian community a church? This paper suggests that a Christian community's effort to fulfill the mission given by Christ suffices to constitute it a Church.

I. MAJOR TRENDS IN ROMAN CATHOLIC THINKING ON THE VALIDITY OF NON-ROMAN CATHOLIC ORDERS

1. THE DECLINE AND FALL OF "APOSTOLICAE CURAE"

What is most striking about current Roman Catholic theological discussions concerning the validity of Anglican Orders is the degree to which the issues raised by *Apostolicae Curae* have ceased to be central to the debate. Controversies concerning the validity of Archbishop Parker's consecration, the sacramental intention of the Ordinal of 1552, Archbishop Cranmer's Eucharistic doctrine, and the make-up of the 1896 Commission seem to have little interest today for Roman Catholic theologians in their consideration of Anglican Orders. In years past this was surely not the case.

There seem to be two reasons for this. The first of these is that the issues raised by that papal document have now been thoroughly explored in a scholarly way in the works of Francis Clark, John Jay Hughes and Edward P. Echlin. Clark[1] offered the best Roman Catholic argument against the validity of Anglican Orders, and presented his case with thoroughness and scholarship. Hughes,[2] after an equally careful examination of the historical evidence and the arguments marshalled by Clark in defense of the judgment of *Apostolicae Curae*, demonstrated convincingly, if not conclusively, that the evidence in support of validity outweighs the arguments adduced by the papal commission.

Echlin[3] in his study of the Anglican Eucharist shows that from the time of the Reformation to the present there has been a steady convergence of both Anglican and Roman Catholic theologies of the Eucharist, and that, given the conflict and confusion of the sixteenth century, it is dangerous to label Cranmer's eucharistic doctrine as heretical. His study generally supports the conclusions of Hughes. If nothing else, the work of Hughes and Echlin has shown that "the historical evidence alone does not permit a firm verdict either in favor of Anglican Orders or against them."[4]

The second reason why *Apostolicae Curae* is seemingly of little interest is that the ground of discussion has shifted significantly. The understanding of orders subjacent to *Apostolicae Curae* and the controversies that succeeded it is a theology of orders bent on explaining the origin, nature, transmission and consequences of the power to celebrate the Eucharistic sacrifice. Orders is narrowly conceived as priesthood, cultic power. Apostolic Succession is the means by which this power is transmitted from one generation of hierarchs to another. It is a canonical mechanism, the gears of which are forged in terms of sacramental form, liturgical rites, ministerial intention and genealogical legitimacy.

The biblical, liturgical and theological movements which issued in Vatican II spelled the end of this theology. The inadequacy of the "traditional" theology of orders has led Roman Catholic theologians to rethink the meaning of ministry and priesthood in the Church, and to begin to develop a theology of ministry within an ecclesiological and eschatological context. It is in terms of this renewed and ecumenical theology of ministry that Roman Catholic theologians now strive to evaluate Anglican Orders.

Thus not only has the historical approach to resolving the question of the validity of Anglican Orders been found wanting, but also the theological understanding of orders represented by *Apostolicae Curae* is now generally recognized as inadequate not only for evaluating Anglican Orders, but even for understanding Roman Catholic Orders.

2. Some New Approaches to the Question of Validity

The new approaches to the question of the validity of Anglican Orders are basically ecclesiological, inspired by Vatican II's recognition of the ecclesial value of other Christian Churches.[5] The basic argument, stated with considerable oversimplification, is that a Christian community cannot be a Church without a ministry — and ultimately without a Eucharistic ministry. Consequently, if in a non-Roman Catholic Christian community, one can recognize the basic structure of the Church, then it must have a true and effective ministry, and thus a ministry that can be recognized by the Roman Catholic Church.

106

Presuppositions

Daniel O'Hanlon[6] summarizes the basic presuppositions common to the new approaches in these five points:

1. A wide variety of Church orders and forms of ministry existed in the Church prior to the generalized acceptance of the monarchical episcopate in the third century.

2. The declarations of ecumenical councils are historically conditioned, polemically oriented, partial and incomplete, necessary but provisional.

3. The Church of Christ is not simply identical with the Roman Catholic Church but rather "subsists in the Catholic Church."[7]

4. Theologians must think in historical, dynamic and eschatological terms, see the Church as the pilgrim people of God, accept that given systems of Church order are provisional, and recognize that a variety of Church orders that would be mutually acceptable is not ruled out by the nature of the Church.

5. The sacrament of order should not be understood exclusively in terms of the *power* to offer the Eucharistic sacrifice, but rather emphasis should be given to the ministerial character of order.

An Ecumenical Understanding of Sacraments

A summary of the position of F. J. Van Beeck[8] does an injustice to the careful and detailed argument that supports his conclusions. He tries to answer two questions:

(1) Can the post-baptismal sacraments celebrated in non-Roman Catholic Christian Churches be true and effective sacraments, even if invalid?

107

(2) Can the ministry which celebrates these sacraments be the presence in non-Roman Catholic Christian Churches of a genuine sacrament of order?

For Van Beeck, validity is a juridical concept signifying "no more (and no less) than the juridical claim to ecclesiastical recognition."[9] He distinguishes validity of ministry from its true and actual effectiveness. The norms of law which serve as criteria for judgments of validity, in spite of the efforts of the lawmaker to provide for all possible situations, do not in fact apply in an extraordinary situation, "in which *ex supposito* there is good faith, but in which the community that celebrates the sacrament is in an emergency situation owing to the fact that its normal ecclesiastical institutions are upset."[10] In this kind of extraordinary situation "one simply cannot even raise the question of validity or invalidity of sacraments and ministry. The question cannot be raised because for this situation no specific concrete norm has been articulated and expressed by the community."[11] Consequently, sacraments and ministry celebrated by a Christian community *existing* in an emergency situation may indeed be true and effective sacraments. The judgment concerning the value and effectiveness of these sacraments and the ministry that celebrates them would be prior to and independent of any eventual judgment concerning their validity:

When a group of Christians gets somehow isolated from the normal Church order without the prospect of speedy normalization of the legal status, it may be asked whether in such a situation the rule of law does not drop out as the standard of sacramental activity altogether.

The ante-juridical, vital foundations of law, on

which the legal system has continued to rely while it did apply, are laid bare. In this hypothesis the isolated *ecclesiola,* in virtue of Christ's presence, could celebrate its sacraments administered by those who in this particular congregation take the burden of ministry upon themselves in view of their spontaneous ability to serve as leaders. In such cases, we would like to suggest, the community could claim a truly sacramental character for these celebrations on the strength of *the diaconal ministry itself plus the possibility for this ministry to be recognized as authentic.*[12]

He summarizes his hypothesis in the following terms:
For a rite to be a true sacrament if administered by a baptized Christian who does not stand in the Apostolic Succession (but who does stand in the Apostolic Tradition) it is required that besides ecclesial background and intention of doing what the Church does, there be found *bona fides* and a protracted extraordinary situation. The latter makes it possible for the sacrament to be administered *praeter ordinem,* whereas the former sees to it that this *praeter ordinem* is not in fact a *contra ordinem,* and so, *ex supposito, contra Ecclesiam.* In spite of ecumenism the Reformed Churches are not subject to the church order of the Roman Church; on the other hand, their very ecumenism bears witness to the fact that they do no longer intend to celebrate the sacraments in an antithetical spirit. Thus our hypothesis can be finally formulated: in view of the extraordinary situation, the *bona fides,* and the authenticity of the *diakonia,* supported by the faith and the ec-

109

clesial character of the community, the ministry of (the Word and) the sacraments as exercised by Protestant ministers may in terms of the Roman Catholic Church order be qualified as recognizable as an extraordinary ministry.[13]

Still even this hypothesis does not respond satisfactorily to the question of whether or not the extraordinary ministry exercised in non-Roman Catholic Christian Churches is a genuine ministry, the actual presence of the sacrament of order in Reformed Churches.

In attempting to respond to this question, Van Beeck submits the following three points:

1. The competence of the minister is not a separate, "extrinsic" condition for the celebration of a sacrament . . . It is *the Church* that celebrates the sacraments *per ministerium ministrorum Ecclesiae,* whose Church membership gets a special direction and point by their having been ordained
. . . .

2. The *bona fide* extraordinary celebration of a sacrament does not change the sacrament; in extraordinary celebrations, therefore, the same sacraments are celebrated as in the ordinary ones. In both cases it is the Church that in faith celebrates and realizes its salvation.

3. If and when a Church in good faith, i.e, not antithetically, celebrates its sacraments through the ministry of a body of ministers as specified by the church order, then — provided the Church order meets the requirements of the episcopal structure of the ministry — not only the sacraments thus celebrated, but also the ministry itself

110

is recogniz*able* as sacramental, *i.e.*, as the Sacrament of Order.[14]

Van Beeck's conclusions are presented as hypotheses and suggestions, and as such are carefully nuanced. They, nevertheless, constitute a theologically sound approach that must be taken into account by Roman Catholic ecumenists in their study of the sacraments and ministry of other Christian Churches. In addition, they provide a ready theological basis for the recognition of the validity of Anglican Orders, as Van Beeck himself suggests.[15]

Ways of Validating Ministry

Kilian McDonnell,[16] using an approach similar to that of Van Beeck, argues that in fact there are three ways of validating ministry: ritual validation, charismatic validation and ecclesiological validation.

"Ritual validation," he says, "is the process by which one determines the verity of a sacrament by inquiring whether the person acting was sacramentally ordained or consecrated, whether the canonically approved form, material and gestures were faithfully adhered to, and whether the intention of the person conferring or confecting the sacrament had the intention of Christ as proposed by the Church."[17]

He states that it is commonly assumed in the Roman Catholic Church that the only way in which ministry can be validated is by ritual validation. However, McDonnell finds that the evidence for this assumption is lacking. It is not supported by the New Testament understanding of ministry. The notion of apostolic succession implicit in the theory of ritual validation is a narrowing of a more biblical and traditional concept of

111

apostolicity. The history of the Church provides numerous examples of non-bishops ordaining priests. The traditional distinction between bishops and priests may in fact be a canonical and disciplinary distinction rather than theological, since even Trent did not affirm that the distinction was *jure divino*.

"Charismatic validation is the process by which one determines the validity of ministry and its sacramental acts by proceeding from the suppositions of a charismatic church order such as obtained at Corinth."[18] Among these suppositions, McDonnell pays particular attention to *four*:

1. Charismatic ministry has validity only in a community of faith, where it has the checks of other gifts, such as a community exercise of discernment of spirits (I Corinthians 12:10; 14:29).[19]
2. It would further presuppose "the original witness and original commission of the Apostles."[20] A charismatic ministry would have to stand within the apostolic succession, which means apostolic faith, life and authority.
3. It would presuppose faith in the Gospel, the reception of Baptism and the priesthood of all believers.
4. Finally, though the charismatic ministry differs from an appointed ministry precisely in the fact that it is exercised without a special ritualized commission, both ministries ultimately rest their claim to effectiveness on the gift of the Spirit.

The point that McDonnell makes is not that a charismatically validated ministry is an ideal, or even a desirable form of ministry in the Church, but that:

> were one to grant that the order of the Pauline churches was that of a charismatic ministry rather

112

than an appointed and ordained ministry (keeping in mind the problem posed by Philippians 1:1), and supposing that this style of ministry was set aside for quite valid and historical and pastoral reasons, and further supposing that the Church accommodated the ministry of her apostolic commission and faith to meet the changed situation, then the question can be asked: If the community of faith set aside a valid expression of apostolic life and ministry for historical and pastoral reasons, is it not possible for the community of faith to re-discover and re-admit this valid charismatic ministry for historical and pastoral reasons?[21]

"Ecclesiological validation is a theological process which proceeds from the nature of the Church and its presence in a community of faith to a recognition of true ministry."[22]

This approach to the validation of ministries received considerable support from Vatican II's *Constitution on the Church*[23] and the *Decree on Ecumenism*,[24] which constitutes the first recognition on the part of the Roman Catholic Church of even the possibility that non-Roman Catholic Christian Churches of the West may indeed enjoy ecclesial status.

Basically, the argument is that where there is a true manifestation of the Church there must of necessity be a true ministry. The ground of this argument is that the Church is the sacrament of Christ, the *Ursakrament*, the primal sacramental reality. "We have a sacrament when the Church particularizes her sacramental nature in those moments of the life of a Christian which are decisive for salvation."[25] In fact, whenever the Church

113

actualizes her sacramental nature, the sacrament of orders is operative, and, consequently, "the validity of ministry should not be attached to a specific form of ministry in an absolute and exclusive manner, for instance, the ministerial commission received by episcopal laying on of hands. Valid ministry is rather attached to the meaning and nature of the Church . . . That form of ministry is good and acceptable which realizes that which Christ meant his church to be."[26] The Church must have ministry, but the particular forms that ministry takes in diverse historical situations are provisional.

In many ways, the arguments of Van Beeck and McDonnell in favor of a new approach to assaying the authenticity of the sacramental ministry in non-Roman Catholic Christian Churches cover much the same ground, present the same evidence, and use the same theological principles, even though each orders his argument in a slightly different way.

Their conclusions are likewise similar. Both insist that the question of whether or not a given Church's ministry is truly sacramental cannot be answered by reference to apostolic succession, conceived in a narrow, canonical sense.

Both insist that if a Christian community is truly a church, *it* is the Sacrament of Christ's saving action and presence in history, and that when the Church particularizes its sacramental nature in actions decisive for salvation, these actions are true sacraments. Both argue that though an Order is necessary for the Church, the particular form of church order now in force in the Roman Catholic Church is not normative, that is, necessarily constituent of what it means to be the Church of God.

Though Van Beeck accepts the correctness of *Apostolicae Curae*, he insists that it leaves untouched the question as to whether Anglican orders are valid or not today.[27] Unlike McDonnell, Van Beeck holds that among the conditions that the ministry of a given church must meet in order to be recognizable as itself a sacrament, and not simply an extraordinary ministry, is that the church have an episcopal structure. This is because the episcopal structure is prototypical and normative, for the bishops stand in the place of the Apostles and it is through the episcopal structure that the apostolic tradition is passed on.[28]

Edward Echlin,[29] in an article on the validity of Anglican Orders, argues from the basic position of Van Beeck. He states that in fact the Anglican Communion is a true church of God, even if there is some irregularity in the episcopal succession. Given the fact that in addition there is now substantial agreement on eucharistic doctrine, he sees no reason to deny validity to Anglican Orders.

Finally, it is interesting to note that it was on the basis of ecclesiological validation that in the Lutheran/Catholic Dialogues, the Catholic theologians recommended that serious consideration be given to the recognition of Lutheran orders, and this in spite of the fact that Lutherans do not claim apostolic succession in ministerial office, but rather apostolicity in doctrine.[30]

II. SOME REFLECTIONS ON CHURCH AND MINISTRY

The *Decree on Ecumenism* names some of the ecclesial realities present in the separated Christian communities of the West.[31] *The Constitution on the Church* designates separated Christian communities as churches.[32] Nevertheless, the documents seem to regard the ecclesial nature of separated Christian Churches in the West as incomplete and imperfect. Consequently, even if the ecclesiological approach to the validation of ministries in non-Catholic Christian Churches is employed, the Roman Catholic Church could indeed judge that the ministry was true, but incomplete and imperfect. It is possible that the imperfections in the ecclesial nature of a given Church could render its Eucharistic ministry invalid.

The new approach to the validation of the ministry of separated Christian Churches of the West ultimately depends on whether or not they manifest to a sufficient degree the presence of the true Church of Christ. If the ecclesiological approach to the validity of ministry is to be useful in ecumenical dialogue, some thought must be given to the ways and means by which to establish the fact that a given Christian community does in fact possess sufficient ecclesial status. The following paragraphs contain some rather wild speculations intended not so much to present solutions to this question, but rather to stimulate imaginative discussion of possible approaches.

How do we evaluate the ecclesial "quality" of a given Church? Is it simply a question of comparing confessional statements, forms of church order, liturgical formularies and ethical standards? Do we establish a list of *sine qua non* ecclesial elements which must be present before a Christian community can be recognized as a Church of Christ? And how do we establish that a given ecclesial element is truly essential? What criterion do we use?

Or is there perhaps another way? Rather than draw

116

up a profile of what a Christian community must possess in the way of faith, doctrine, order, worship, and ethical codes in order to be truly a Church of Christ (surely we recognize that any such definition of Church would be heavily conditioned by the history of the defining Church), perhaps it would be preferable to establish criteria that would be admittedly less sophisticated from a theological point of view but also closer to life.

It seems possible to say that wherever there is a recognizable concrete community of believers gathered and organized to carry out the mission that Christ confided to his Church and which does in fact strive to submit its life to the guidance of Sacred Scripture, there the Church of God is truly present. The Church exists for the sake of the mission confided in her. The mission calls the Church into being and determines her nature and internal organization. What is the mission? Mark's Gospel states it simply as: "Go into the whole world and proclaim the good news to all creation."[33] Vatican II expresses the same idea in terms of the Kingdom: "to proclaim and establish among all peoples the Kingdom of Christ."[34] But no matter how expressed, its fundamental nature and demands are witnessed to in Sacred Scripture. The simplicity of these statements conceals the extreme difficulty inherent in describing this mission with exactitude. Every word is pregnant with the whole history of God's relationship with man. The material content of the mission develops as the community called into existence by it makes its way in history. However, from a strictly formal point of view, the mission is to continue the saving presence and action of Christ by proclaiming in word and deed the good news of salvation that the Kingdom of God is at hand.[35] This mission calls into existence a human community, which by means of its own existence and action can continue to manifest the saving presence and action of Christ as the beginning of the last times leading ineluctably to the full realization of the Kingdom promised in Christ.

Now the whole thrust of Vatican Council II was to insist that even though the mission of the Church is ever the same, and that even though the human community called into existence by this mission enjoys a similar perdurance as long as the mission remains not fuly realized, the ways by which the Church organizes its existence and action in view of its mission must continually change with the changes taking place in the concrete historical moments in which it must exist and act. The Church is a human institution. It is made up of men, organized by men for the sake of men. It exists in time and space, and is subject to the laws and principles operative in all human institutions. This, of course, does not exclude the fact that this institution has a divine origin, is graced, supported and guided by the Holy Spirit, and is itself a sacramental reality, destined to an eschatological fulfillment beyond the limits of man's endeavors. On the other hand, the religious significance of this institution should not lead us either in thought or speech to dehumanize it by imagining that because of either its origin or spiritual significance it escapes the dynamics and limitations of human institutions in general. A cursory reading of the history of the Church is illustrative of this fact.

It would not be improbable to suggest that many Christian communities would not be able to meet the ecclesial standards that characterize the Roman Catholic Church in the latter half of the twentieth century.

There are Christian communities whose Trinitarian and Christological doctrines are at best primitive and ill-formed. Could even the Church of the Acts, or of Corinth, or of Antioch meet these contemporary standards? The Roman Catholic Church, the Orthodox Church and the major Christian Churches that spring from the sixteenth-century reform are the products of almost two millenia of doctrinal and ecclesiological development. These developments may indeed be authentically evangelical, the fruits of the Spirit's presence, but it also seems possible that Christian communities whose theology, church order, worship, and ethical codes show considerably less development are victims of historical situations, cultural limitations, isolation brought on by political divisions, and other like circumstances (including the schisms and divisions which have wracked the Church from its very beginnings). Is an underdeveloped Christian community by that very fact less a Church of Christ than a Christian community that witnesses to extensive development? In other words, is the fact of development the *sine qua non* for ecclesial status?

As we argued above, it is the Church's mission that calls her into existence and determines her nature and internal organization. In fact, however, the way in which the mission determines the Church's nature and internal organization is subject to the laws of human institutions and conditioned by historical situations. The material content of the mission develops as the community makes its way in history, but this development too is conditioned by history. Consequently, the understanding that one Christian community may have of that mission may differ widely from that of another Christian community, and this difference will surely affect the self-understanding of the two communities, but so long as both are recognizable concrete communities of believers, gathered and organized to continue the mission Christ gave His Church, namely, to proclaim and establish among all peoples the kingdom of Christ and of God, then it would seem that both are truly Churches of Jesus Christ.

On the basis of this hypothesis, any recognizable concrete community of believers gathered and organized to proclaim and establish the kingdom of Christ and of God which does in fact strive to live in accord with Sacred Scripture, even though its understanding of that faith may be sadly inadequate by some contemporary standards, would indeed be a true Church of God.

Perhaps we should therefore abandon the categories of complete and incomplete when speaking of the ecclesial nature of a Christian community and instead posit their full ecclesial reality on the basis of those minimal criteria sketched above, and consider differences in doctrine, worship, order, and ethics as fundamentally a question of stages in development, recognizing that the history of each community has had a profound effect on how it is a Church of Christ.

Where does the ministry fit into this conception of the Church? What is its role in the Church?

Like any human community, the Church must be ordered, structured and organized in terms of its goals. The nature and character of the structure or organization may vary with times and places — and indeed must vary to meet the demands imposed by its mission in a variety of historical situations.

Ministry is essentially the ordering function in the Church. It is the particular service of order which renders the Church capable of responding to her mission. The nature of this service, the ways in which it is performed, the modalities of its exercise are a function of a number of factors. Primary among these factors are the following: (1) the Church's mission; (2) the nature of the community as it is determined by the mission; (3) the historical moment in which the Church must carry out its mission.

The ordering service which ministry renders in the Church is not purely and simply a service rendered to the community, entirely at the behest of the community. Rather, ministry orders the community precisely by calling upon the community to be faithful to its mission. Since the community exists only in terms of its mission, a ministry which would allow the community to neglect its reason for existence would render it a disservice. There are then in the ministry several dimensions: ministry represents the community, but it also stands over against the community to render judgment on the community to the world; it also represents Christ to the community.[36]

Traditionally, the ordering function performed by ministry in the Church has been described in terms of the three-fold task of teaching, governing, and sanctifying, or as an exercise of the prophetic, royal and priestly powers of the ministry. However, a more recent formulation of this ordering function by Fr. Schillebeeckx[37] seems to be preferable. He speaks of four basic services that the ministry performs in ordering the Church for its mission:

(1) To lead and guide the community so that it recognizes Christ as its only Lord;

(2) to serve faithfully the Word of God
   — by preaching and teaching in accord with the apostolic faith;
   — by leading the community's sacramental celebrations of the Word;
   — by administering the "consolation of the Scriptures" (Romans 15:4) in exhortation and admonition;

(3) to lead the community in that love which seeks justice for all men, i.e., to promote the concern which the community should have for man in his concrete historical situation (normally this implies the role of critic of both the community and society);

(4) to initiate others in the offices of the Church.

These, of course, simply outline the functions of the ordering service that ministry renders in the Church. These functions flow from the mission given by Christ which calls the Church into being. How in a given situation this ordering service is itself organized, depends on the concrete historical situations in which the Church is called upon to fulfill its mission, and how the Church at a given stage of development understands its mission and thus itself.

As for the validity of ministry, so long as it is the ministry of a Christian community recognized as a Church of Christ, it would be a true and authentic ministry. That ministry's effectiveness would, however, be limited by the Church's understanding of its mission, and consequently by its own self-understanding. Assuming that a given Church develops a conception of the Eucharist that we as Roman Catholics would consider orthodox, it would also seem that by the very fact of development, that Church's ministry would become what we as Roman Catholics consider a valid Eucharistic ministry, and could in fact be recognized as such. Nor would such recognition necessarily require that the Roman Catholic Church recognize all the sacramental acts of that ministry as valid. Ministry must always be seen as function of a Church's self-understanding, as determined by the way it perceives the mission Christ has committed to it.

Conclusion

These may indeed be wild speculations. Nevertheless, they seem to be founded on the principles inherent in the notion of ecclesiological validation, but applied in the light of our contemporary recognition of the intrinsic historicity of the Church and our knowledge of it as a developing reality.

There does not seem to be any serious reason for not granting full ecclesial recognition to most of the separated Churches of the West. No one who has experienced the life and vitality of these Churches can reasonably doubt that they are Christian communities organized and gathered to proclaim and establish among all nations the Kingdom of God and of Christ and that they do in fact strive to live the apostolic faith as they undersand it from Sacred Scripture. As to the validity of their ministries, these judgments could be made on the basis of agreements as to the meaning and value of various sacramental acts celebrated in these Churches. Where, as in the case of the Anglican and Lutheran Churches, there is between these Churches and the Roman Catholic Church substantial agreement on Eucharistic doctrine, there is no solid reason why the Eucharistic ministries of each should not be recognized as valid by the others.

V

PAPACY IN THE CHURCH OF THE FUTURE

A Roman Catholic View

by

HENRY G. J. BECK

SUMMARY

On August 25, 1971, Pope Paul VI affirmed that all church authority, papal included, is "a service . . . for the benefit of those who are in need of it. Its style must be evangelical."

The contention of this paper is that the authentic papal ministry is that depicted in Matthew 16, Luke 22 and John 21, which is one of faith and love, excluding all domination and power, extending to all Christians, involving sacrifice and pain, authoritative and central within the church, supportive of others while supported itself in constant collaboration with the people of God. Such an office commends itself as biblically, ecumenically and theologically sound and viable as visible center of the church universal.

Behind this paper lie three influences: 1) a formal theological education at Rome in the 1930's at a time when scholasticism was dominant and the single Catholic view of the papacy was a strict interpretation of what the First Vatican Council had said on the subject. In retrospect, I recall neither question nor doubt as to the all-sufficiency of the 1870 position on primacy and infallibility;[1] 2) an awareness nurtured by the studies of the 1940's and 1950's that there is a broad biblical dimension to the petrine ministry which must be located within the mystery of Christ and within the mystery of the church;[2] 3) a conviction growing throughout the 1960's and 1970's that any theology which treats of Peter and his office has to be seen against the ecumenical background of the entire christian community.[3]

It is the contention of this essay that a primatial ministry, faithful to the insights of the Gospel, not unfaithful to the teaching of the Vatican I, may emerge in the church of the future in such fashion as to serve well a christendom to which organic unity has been restored. I cannot pretend that all Roman Catholics have caught this vision. I do not suggest that all desire this direction. But I do contend that the view of the papal potential sketched in the following pages does not deviate from Catholic orthodoxy. Were it to become really operative (and it is the prayer of the writer that it will), the papal office would commend itself to all christians as biblically, ecumenically and theologically sound and viable as a visible center of the world church.

I suspect that in the present climate of deep concern for christian unity, an interpretation of the petrine office which accords with the values of the New Testament and which holds ecumenical promise has within itself its major commendation. Quite apart from whether Peter actually played such a role as will here be depicted, Christians might well consider the need that we have *now*, for this type of ministry. But lest my own biases show inadvertantly, I set out now my personal convictions that 1) Christ did indeed bestow this function upon the man Peter rather than make observations concerning characteristics following from faith in Him;[4] 2) the petrine ministry is a constituent of the church of

Christ and is destined to endure as long as the church persists;[5] 3) there is an historical link between Peter's own office and the succession of the Roman bishops.[6]

To those who reject any or all of the foregoing three propositions, it can still be proposed that given the state of christian unity/disunity today and in the near future, there is high value in the activation (or reactivation) within the church of a central ministry comparable to the petrine office here understood in biblical and ecumenical context. One will hardly fault the church of the future if it uses a universal pastoral ministry built upon Gospel grounds.[7] And to call such a ministry a papal ministry is only to recognize that factually since the third century none but the Roman popes have ever laid claim to a like position within the world-wide church.

It is well known that the First Vatican Council (1869-70) saw the basis for a papal and petrine primacy in three New Testament texts: Matthew 16:16-19, Luke 22:24-32, John 21:15-19.[8] The Matthean text especially has a long history of citation in support of a Roman primacy.[9] Upon these and about these texts Vatican I built its explanation of papal ministry and thought to find support for its position in the teaching of the earlier (western) ecumenical councils of II Lyons (1274) and Florence (1439).[10]

It is my conviction that, despite the legalistic framework and historical shortsightedness manifest at Vatican I, a pastoral ministry confided to a single individual and lived humbly within the dimensions of Matthew 16, Luke 22 and John 21 (as depicted below) may legitimately make demands upon all christians. A petrine ministry so exercised, I contend, can bestow wide benefit upon the whole church of God.

> Simon Peter answered and said: You are the
> Christ, the Son of the Living God.
> And Jesus answering said to him: Blessed are
> you, Simon Bar-Jona: because flesh and blood
> has not revealed it to you, but my Father who is
> in heaven.
> And I say to you: You are Peter and on this rock
> I will build my church and powers of death shall
> not prevail against it.
> And I will give you the keys of the kingdom of
> heaven. And whatever you bind on earth shall be
> bound in heaven, and whatever you loose on earth
> shall be loosed in heaven. — Matthew 16:16-19

To take first the data of Matthew 16:16-19, the ministry therein envisioned as Peter's is marked by: A) *an especial witness to the uniqueness of the Lord Jesus* ("You are the Christ, the Son of the living God.") which has historically involved an eagerness beyond that of the fellow disciples to put itself at the disposition of the Master[11] and a readiness, above that of others, to proclaim the Lord and His ways both to believer and non-believer.[12] In concrete terms, such a ministry is involved not with administrative details but with the discovery and attestation of the place of Jesus in relationship to the problems faced by humans both in the church and in the world;[13] B) *a rock-like quality whose firmness brings strength and support to the rest of the community* ("You are Peter and on this rock I will build my church and powers of death shall not prevail against it."). The function of the rock foundation in sustaining the edifice reared upon it is otherwise noted in the sayings of the Lord.[14] Here He would seem to be referring to a single, solid individual upon whom the brotherhood ("church") comes to rely successfully in its struggle with forces of evil. "There was to be leadership and authority in the church, and Peter would have a crucial role in laying its foundation. The church was not to live in anarchy but in unity and with order adapted to the living situation, and Peter had his basic place in this original development and work of the church;"[15] C) *a key position which is at one and the same time visibly representative of Jesus to His people and authoritative among the members* ("I will give you the keys of the kingdom of heaven."), vicegerent, vicar as regards the Lord of the establishment, endowed with a directive competence as regards the constituency of the community;[16] D) *power to judge what is licit and illicit in achieving the purposes of the brotherhood, able to formulate the conditions under which the membership is to act* ("Whatever you bind on earth shall be bound in heaven, and whatever you loose on earth shall be loosed in heaven."), thus reproducing within the christian assembly the role of decision-giving exercised by the rabbis under the old covenant.[17]

In this sketch of the ministry found in Matthew, characteristics A), B) and C) are to be seen as personal prerogatives peculiar to the exerciser of the function. Indeed, it may be suggested that preeminent witness to the Lord, rock-like firmness of faith, and vicarial representation of Jesus will be of particular worth to the whole community if they are outstandingly manifest in a single individual who thus inspires the rest of his brethren. But, when taken with characteristic D), another passage in Matthew ("Amen I say to you, whatsoever you shall bind upon earth shall be bound also in heaven: and whatsoever you shall loose upon earth shall be loosed also in heaven.") [18] implies that it is to be a collegial activity exercised in full collaboration among primate, apostolic college and faithful. Details are not spelled out, rather must the everyday exercise of this authority be left to the surge of the life of the people of God. Applications will, no doubt, vary from age to age. There have, admittedly, been periods in the story of the church when the primate prided himself upon a *plenitudo potestatis*. But there has also been recognition of the need and the rightness of the petrine ministry's "sounding out the mind of the church throughout the whole world." [19] It is this latter procedure, extendable simply to all the concerns of the church and mankind, which would seem to me to be indispensable to the petrine office in an age which prizes pluralism and personalism. If Peter is to direct as pastor in such a situation, he must first have been in active consultation with the body of the faithful.

A dispute arose also between them about which should be reckoned the greatest, but he said to them, "Among pagans it is the kings who lord it over them, and those who have authority over them are given the title Benefactor. This must not happen with you. No; the greatest among you must behave as if he were the youngest, the leader as if he were the one who serves. For who is the greater: the one at table or the one who serves? The one at table, surely? Yet here am I among you as one who serves!

You are the men who have stood by me faithfully in my trials; and now I confer a kingdom on you, just as my Father conferred one on me: you will eat and drink at my table in my kingdom, and

you will sit on thrones to judge the twelve tribes
of Israel.

Simon, Simon! Satan, you must know, has got his
wish to sift you all like wheat; but I have prayed
for you, Simon, that your faith may not fail, and
once you have recovered, you in your turn must
strengthen your brothers." — Luke 22:24-32

In the second petrine text, Luke 22:24-32, the Lord
lays down guidelines for the leadership of His church.
It is not to be a domination ("exercise lordship") but a
humble dedication ("the leader as one who serves") and
is to find its exemplar in Jesus' own placing of Himself
at the disposition of His people. He anticipates periods
of severe trial for the collective authority ("that he
might sift *you* like wheat," *you*, plural). For this He
provides in praying for Peter and charging him with the
sustaining and encouraging of the whole brotherhood
("strengthen your brethren"). Here the petrine ministry is seen as supportive; he is to be the stronghold of
the faith.[20] Unique though it is, such an office does not
exclude other consolidating ministries. Peter himself
could call this to the attention of his fellow presbyters:
"Tend the flock of God that is your charge, not by constraint but willingly, not for shameful gain but eagerly,
not as domineering over those in your charge but being
examples to the flock."[21]

After the meal Jesus said to Simon Peter, "Simon,
son of John, do you love me more than these
others do?" He answered, "Yes, Lord, you know I
love you." Jesus said to him, "Feed my lambs." A
second time he said to him, "Simon son of John,
do you love me?" He replied, "Yes, Lord, you
know I love you." Jesus said to him, "Look after

my sheep." Then he said to him a third time,
"Simon son of John, do you love me?" Peter was
upset that he asked him the third time, "Do you
love me?" and said, "Lord, you know everything;
you know I love you." Jesus said to him, "Feed
my sheep."

"I tell you most solemnly, when you were young
you put on your belt and walked where you liked;
but when you grow old you will stretch out your
hands and somebody else will put a belt around
you and take you where you would rather not
go." In these words he indicated the kind of death
by which Peter would give glory to God. After
this he said, "Follow me."   — John 21:15-19

Both the Matthean and the Lucan passages envision
a special faith-role for the petrine office; in the third
text, John 21:15-19, the stress is upon love.[22] As a consequence of his love for Jesus (the affirmation of which
is thrice solicited), Peter is thrice commanded to assume
towards the Lord's people the responsibility of shepherd
("feed my lambs . . . look after my sheep . . . feed my
sheep")[23] Clearly it is a case of providing for needs and
preserving from harm. The Old Testament knows the
metaphor.[24] So also does the New Testament where, in
John 10, Jesus portrays Himself as shepherd.[25] Given the
Lord's own statement: "I lay down my life for the
sheep" (John 10:15) and His intimation (John 21:18-
19) that Peter will be asked to do the same, the shepherding demanded of Peter can only be viewed as a
self-sacrificing ministry.

Cumulatively, the ministry confided to Peter in the
three New Testament passages just examined emerges

as one of faith and of love, excluding all domination and power, extending to all the household of the faith, involving sacrifice and pain, authoritative and central within the church, supportive of others and yet supported itself by the collaboration of the people of God. There is no hint that it is to be insensitive to needs, no indication that it is to draw only from itself. In it and through it, Jesus is to live and to nourish His people.

Theological summaries on the petrine-papal office are readily available.[26] So, too, are studies of papal history.[27] But it takes little expertise to recognize that the papacy has grown with history. One does not expect the role accorded the petrine ministry in the third century by St. Cyprian of Carthage's *De unitate ecclesiae*[28] to be identical with that claimed in 1302 by Pope Boniface VIII's *Unam sanctam.*[29] Even limiting oneself to the medieval period, the evidence for development and change in papal authority and structures is beyond all question.[30]

This factor of development suggests — indeed, demands — that in the church of the future the fashioning of the petrine ministry will follow very different lines than it has hitherto. At Vatican I, the post-tridentine vision of the papacy pictured a "full and supreme power of jurisdiction over the whole church . . . ordinary and immediate . . . over each and every church . . . over each and every shepherd and faithful member."[31] How will the vision be focussed in the church of tomorrow?

I suspect that the term *jurisdiction* has had its day and that others — *ministry, office, service* — will be taking its place. More and more the petrine function will be pastoral and inspirational rather than governmental. Progressively, the biblical dimensions we have seen in Matthew, Luke and John will supplant the juridic concepts that have come to us from the Constantinian age. Since these scriptural underpinnings have been so much a part of the papal claims in the past, it should not be difficult for theologians to remain within the tradition and yet present the primatial office as a service to all the servants of God, as a shepherding of all Christ's sheep.

Neither the New Testament nor the history of the church prescribes the specifics of this service and shepherding. The forms have been as varied in papal annals as they have anywhere else. For most of christian antiquity, the petrine ministry was almost exclusively a center for appeal. Later, as the church came to value centralization and uniformity, the papal office took on the coloration of another period. Still later, since Vatican II, a return to decentralization has begun to be seen. In this climate of pluralism, self-determination and freedom, there is nothing which precludes the papacy from functioning with such a value system.

Once the point is made that the petrine ministry is a service to all the brotherhood, extending to shepherds and sheep ("ordinary and immediate"), then its commitment to the community requires a flexibility and adaptability whereby it can respond to the different needs of different ages. Conceivably, some periods are best served in an atmosphere of paternalistic guidance. Then, the petrine ministry is well advised to prescribe even minor details. Other ages — ours included — prize consultation and shared decision-making. In such a context, the primatial office best benefits the church by the wide use of popular participation in delineating the objectives to be achieved.

I would stress that a like flexibility is not a question of political expediency. It should not be a reluctant papacy which accepts collegiality because arbitrary rule has become impossible. Rather, the very principle of the petrine ministry is that it is in the church to further the growth of christians. It is there to serve, not to be served. All its efficiency is measured by the way in which it helps people to develop in Christ. This ministry is healthy when it aids the community to move to maturity; it is deficient when it does not. Peter is Peter when he founds the faith of the people of God, strengthens his brethren, feeds the Lord's sheep. His honor is the adulthood of co-believers.

In the longed-for world church of the future, with the unity once again patent, the petrine ministry will be effective only if it binds the community together. Given the personalism and pluralism which have marked the age in which we live, it may be surmised that the mass of christians can only become a people if their self-determination is respected and fostered. "Sounding out the mind of the church throughout the whole world" (Vatican I) would seem to be indispensable if the assembly of the faithful is to be helped to work energetically towards Gospel goals.

Precisely because the mechanics of this ministry are not specified in scripture, possibilities will present themselves in one age which are not to hand in another. The early church was a period largely of regional solutions to problems which affected the brotherhood. The middle ages in the west moved towards a common canon law. At both stages, the papal ministry reacted in appreciably different ways. In today's situation, with national episcopal conferences coming into prominence, it would again be possible for the primatial office to conceive of its role as that of encouraging local decisions at grassroot levels. This would not deny its primacy. Rather would it be clear that this ministry of Peter is "ordinary and immediate" since it is supportive of every judgment made by the church at every level of its life.

This is not to deny that the church of the future will lack world-wide vision. Already a world synod of bishops has come into existence to provide the episcopate of the six continents an opportunity, with Peter, to set common goals. Further enlargement of this concept through international organs representative of clergy, religious and laity will give other segments of the christian community a like possibility. Fostering these, though not manipulating them, will supply the petrine ministry ample field in which to demonstrate its solicitude for each and every church and for each and every shepherd and faithful member.

I am inclined to believe that if Peter walks this path of nurturing decision-making through all the strata of ecclesiastical life, the patent evangelical nature of his ministry will dispel the fears of those who saw and see the papal office as a denaturing of the Gospel. And for christians who have been uneasy with a claim to apostolic succession,[32] the lived experience of an apostolic pastoral concern may well spur them to rethinking their anxieties.

Will papal infallibility effectively prevent the petrine ministry from acting as a unifying force in the church of the future? At the moment, there is wide-ranging debate as to the meaning of the term. Are we dealing with a claim that certain proclamations of church and papacy are divinely safeguarded as to their truth quality? Or are we saying only that neither the community nor Peter will ever fail in witnessing to the faith?[33] Whatever the answer (already nuances have been advanced which escaped earlier commentators), it will be needful to underscore the nexus between Peter and the church. Vatican I was not unaware of this, for it explicitly placed the exercise of papal infallibility within the framework of inquiry and consultation of the whole church.[34] It is this linking of papal teaching to the teaching of the church which will facilitate the work of future theologians. I suspect that a reunited christendom which finds a consensus on the truth-value of church teaching will be able to extend that agreement to the area of papal doctrinal competence. Or to put it another way: whatever quality will be assigned the teaching of the universal church will be seen also to apply to the teaching of the petrine ministry functioning within and through the church.

No man alive can assess with assurance the development of the church in the years ahead. No man can say whether a Peter will arise who as a "true believer who truly serves his fellow men and who has a true power to convince them . . . possesses a gift for religious leadership, an understanding of what constitutes a world church and an insight into the basic needs of mankind."[35] But if he does, the simple pastoral ministry in Matthew 16, Luke 22 and John 21 exercised by him should be seen as extraordinarily relevant to the whole church, extraordinarily suitable to its time, possessed of a future which holds hope and promise not only for the church but for the whole of humanity.[36]

An Anglican Perspective

by

J. ROBERT WRIGHT

SUMMARY

Sixteenth century Anglican views of the papacy were the
products of Reformation polemic and controversy. A contrast
with those of the twentieth century suggests evolution from an
"anti-papal" stance to one which today may at least be described as "non-papal." Especially since Vatican Council II,
there are some Anglican leaders who are expressing considerable interest in the possibilties that some limited form of papal
leadership may offer to the one church of the future. Contemporary Roman Catholic views of the papacy, though rather narrowly concentrated on the infallibility question, reveal a wide
spectrum of doctrinal pluralism presently tolerated, and in particular the toleration of interpretation not wholly incompatible
with some recent Anglican thought. As both Anglicans and
Roman Catholics look at tomorrow's church, it would seem that
they will have different, rather than contradictory, expressions
of the petrine office, both of which may affirm the pope as chief
pastor of the Christian family.

This paper has three objectives: 1) to contrast some
Anglican views of the papacy in the sixteenth century
with some on the eve of the Second Vatican Council and
in even more recent times; 2) to survey some contemporary Roman Catholic views of the papacy; and 3) to
sketch some of the contours in which both Anglicans
and Roman Catholics will have to see the papal office as
they face their futures in a dialogue of rapidly increasing momentum and reciprocity.

(1) Anglican Views

Forged in the furnace of Reformation controversy,

138

the Henrician anti-papal legislation[1] pushed the medieval statutes of *Provisors* and *Praemunire* to their extremes and forced the practical implementation of royal claims that since the fourteenth century for the most part had been theories held in a careful balance of working compromise between king and pope. As the crown began to assume theoretical as well as actual control over the English Church in the 1530's, especially in the areas of ecclesiastical courts, episcopal appointments, and church taxation, the papacy came to be viewed as the major enemy of the English Church in a way that had not been so before.[2] Whether or not the English Church in the middle ages enjoyed a degree of independence from papal authority greater than that of other national provinces (and this is still a subject of scholarly dispute),[3] it is certainly clear that the relative positions of crown and pope in the nation's past history were rewritten at this time to make it seem so.[4] There was indeed a continuity of much traditional catholic faith and practice, and in a paper of this brevity there is no room to assess either the manifold factors causing the English Reformation or the extent to which they were justified, but for present purposes we may conclude by observing that the papal connection was in fact broken and that the pope of Rome bore the major brunt of the polemic.[5] The medieval English tradition was in this way made to seem much more anti-papal than had in fact been the case.[6]

Perhaps not surprising in view of an already incipient Anglican emphasis upon the principle of *lex orandi lex credendi*, this anti-papal polemic found its way into some of the earliest liturgical expressions authorized by the English reformers,[7] and so it is that in the first English Litany (1544) we find the deprecation clause "From the tyranny of the Bysshop of Rome and al hys detestable enormities . . . , Good lord, deliver us." Incorporated into the first and second English prayer books, this clause was not discarded until the third (Elizabethan) book of 1559.[8]

Classical Anglican apologetic soon found its first chief spokesman in the Bishop of Salisbury, John Jewel, who wrote his *Apology of the Church of England* in 1562. The following passage[9] from it is worth quoting for its importance as an influential early example of the Anglican method whereby the Henrician political severance of the papal connection came to be given theological justification on grounds of a patristic golden age.

Tell us, I pray you, good Holy Father, seeing ye do crack so much of all antiquity and boast yourself that all men are bound to you alone, which of all the fathers have at any time called you by the name of the highest prelate, the universal bishop or head of the church? Which of them ever said that both the swords were committed to you? Which of them ever said that you have authority and right to call councils? Which of them ever said that the whole world is your diocese? Which of them, that all bishops have received of your fullness? Which of them, that all power is given to you as well in heaven as in earth? Which of them, that neither kings, nor the whole clergy, nor yet all people together, are able to be judges over you? Which of them, that kings and emperors by Christ's commandment and will do receive authority at your hand? Which of them, that more ample authority is given to you than to the residue of the patriarchs? Which of them, that you are the Lord God? Or that you are not a mere natural man but a certain substance made and grown together of God and man? Which of them, that you are the only headspring of all law? Which of them, that you have power over purgatories? Which of them, that you are able to command the angels of God as you list yourself? Which of them that ever said that you are Lord of lords and the King of kings? We can also go further with you in like sort. What one amongst the whole number of the old bishops and fathers ever taught you either to say private Mass while the people stared on or to lift up the sacrament over your head (In which point consisteth now all your religion); or else to mangle Christ's sacraments and to bereave the people of the one part, contrary to Christ's institution and plain expressed words? But, that we may once come to an end, what one is there of all the fathers which hath taught you to distribute Christ's blood and the holy martyr's merits, and to sell openly as merchandises your pardons and all the rooms and lodgings of purgatory? These men are wont to speak much of a certain secret doctrine of theirs and manifold and sundry readings. Then let them bring forth somewhat now, if they can, that it may appear they have at least read or do know somewhat. They have often stoutly noised in all corners where they went how all the parts of their religion be very old and have been approved not only by the multitude but also by the consent and continual observation of all nations and times.

141

Let them therefore once in their life show this their antiquity. Let them make appear at eye that the things whereof they make such ado have taken so long and large increase. Let them declare that all Christian nations have agreed by consent to this their religion. . . . They have not, good Lord, they have not (I say) those things which they boast they have: they have not that antiquity, they have not that universality, they have not that consent of all places nor of all times.

This strongly negative Anglican view of the papacy can be traced in still other sources of the time, not the least of which is the inaugural lecture of the future Archbishop of Canterbury, John Whitgift, given upon his becoming Lady Margaret Professor of Divinity at Cambridge University in 1563 on the popular theme "The Pope is Antichrist."[10]

Cut off in this rather vitriolic way from any further consideration of the papal obedience, the Anglican theological tradition began to have its own development now, both catholic and reformed, without direct reference to the mainstream of Roman Catholic life and thought. A thorough and careful history of Anglican attitudes towards the papacy from the Reformation to the present, yet to be written and much to be desired,[11] would — I believe — reveal many interesting shifts as well as a persistent evolution. We may note in passing that the seventeenth century divines, although some are much exercised over the problem of infallibility as they see it, on the whole strike a more balanced and at times moderate note.[12] Even the invectives against infallibility penned by such men as William Chillingworth (*A Discourse against the Infallibility of the Roman Church,*

1634?),[13] Jeremy Taylor (*A Dissuasive from Popery*, 1664),[14] Henry Dodwell (1676)[15] and George Hicks (1680),[16] are written with little reference to the actual Roman experience of the post-Tridentine papacy, and it is such works as these that set the tone for an Anglican "case" against the doctrine of infallibiilty long before it was defined at the First Vatican Council of 1870.

The purpose of the present essay being a contrast rather than an exhaustive study, we shall now move past the following centuries, omitting consideration except by title of the papal interests of the Oxford Movement reformers, up to the twentieth century. Here we may see a remarkable conrast to the invectives of former ages, and indeed not a few opinions that can at least be described as irenic. First we may cite a theologian participating in the Malines Conversations of 1921-5, who, it is said, "did not include Anglo-Catholicism amongst his crimes": J. Armitage Robinson, the Dean of Wells, was prepared to accord the Roman see "a general superintendence, a care for the well-being of the churches as a whole," and wished for "much more than a simple primacy of honour" for the pope.[17]

Other Anglican church historians had similar views. B. J. Kidd, Warden of Keble and another Malines theologian, wrote in 1936 of the Roman primacy "it was a primacy of leadership, more than a primacy of honour though less than a primacy of jurisdiction, and the bishop of Rome as occupant of the first apostolic see in Christendom derives from St. Peter and St. Paul, the twin founders in the sense of organizers of the church in Rome, that pre-eminence which has been accorded to him everywhere, always and by all and is still generally recognized as his." H. E. Symmonds, in his study of early relations between the papacy and the episcopate (1939), concluded, "The episcopate was one in essence and ideal. But this unity had its centre in the apostolic see of Rome. This centre . . . is not indeed of such necessity that all cut off from it are by that fact cut off from membership within the Church of Christ. Yet in the eyes of all it was the see to which all Christians looked. . . ." And Dr. T. G. Jalland of Exeter in his Bampton Lectures (1944) observed, "The Roman see was recognized by other churches as possessing from early times, if not from the beginning, an undoubted primacy in the sphere of doctrine at least in the sense of a right to be heard in preference to others . . . the right of the papacy to act as supreme judge in matters of discipline if not traceable so far back as the doctrinal primacy is at least contemporary in respect of its development with the evolution of episcopal jurisdiction."

The present Archbishop of Canterbury, Dr. Michael Ramsey, in his first major theological work (*The Gospel and the Catholic Church*, 1936), struck a note which, perhaps ahead of its day in the climate of the 1930's, nevertheless has a curiously contemporary ring to one who studies the evaluations of the papacy being made in our own time:

It was stated in Chapter V that a Papacy which acted as an organ of the Church's general consciousness and authority in doctrine, and which focused the unity of the one Episcopate might claim to fulfil the tests of true development. And it was further stated in Chapter XI that at certain times in history the Papacy conspicuously failed to do this and has thereby been the means of perverting the real meaning of Catholicism. But this historical fact cannot justify a wholesale refusal to consider the Petrine claims. Other organs in the one Body have had their times of failure and of self-aggrandisement, and we do not therefore conclude that they must be discarded. Hence it seems possible that in the reunited Church of the future there may be a special place for a "*primus-inter-pares*" as an organ of unity and authority. Peter will be needed as well as Paul and Apollos, and like them he will be chastened and repentant.[18]

Finally, the document which is perhaps the nearest thing to a comprehensive and in some way quasi-official statement of Anglican doctrine, the report of the commission appointed by the Archbishops of Canterbury and York entitled *Doctrine in the Church of England* (1938), constructed a very cautious balance in its own conclusions which probably represent, if not the clear hard thinking of some one person like Ramsey, at least an honest evaluation of the total spectrum of Anglican thinking on the papacy at that time: [19]

We are united in holding that the Church of England was right to take the stand which it took in the sixteenth century and is still bound to resist the claims of the contemporary Papacy. The account which we have already given of the nature of spiritual and doctrinal authority supplies in large measure the ground of our conviction on this point. With regard to the Church of the future, some of us look forward to a reunion of Christendom having its centre in a Primacy such as might be found in a Papacy which had renounced certain of its present claims; some, on the other hand, look forward to union by a more federal type of constitution which would have no need for such a Primacy.

By the eve of the Second Vatican Council, then, even in the absence of an exhaustive historical survey, I think we can say that the Anglican view of the papacy had evolved from the consciously "anti-papal" polemic of the sixteenth century to an attitude which in the mid-twentieth century can at least be called "non-papal" by contrast.

And in more recent times since Vatican II, there are indications that this "non-papal" stance has for at least some Anglicans proceeded to an expressed interest in exploring the possibilities that some form of actual papal leadership may offer to the one church of the future. The senior Anglican delegate-observer at Vatican II, Bishop Moorman of Ripon, has made the following comments (1966 and 1967) : [20]

> Whether we like it or not, things can never be the same again (*since the Second Vatican Council*). In the ecumenical world Rome has, to some extent, taken the initiative, and the question now being asked is: 'What is the rest of Christendom going to do about it? How does this apply to the Anglican Communion?' The Anglican Communion began as a 'national' Church — the Church of the English people —and, to some extent, it still preserves that characteristic, although it has spread all over the world. Many would like to continue as such; but the days of 'national Churches' are over, and the Anglican Communion will probably have to join up sooner or later with one or other of the main 'families' or groups of

Christians. There are three such 'families' — Roman, Orthodox, and Reformed. Here it is interesting to note that, roughly speaking, of every ten people in the world, six are non-Christian, two are Roman Catholic, one is Orthodox, and one Reformed (that is, Lutheran, Anglican, Calvinist, Methodist, Baptist, etc.). With which of these three 'families' should the Anglican Communion eventually find its home? . . . To a great many Anglicans any idea of union with Rome seems quite out of the question. We have had so many years of bitterness, misunderstanding and fear that the obstacles would seem insuperable. But the Vatican Council has made a big difference. Rome is now very anxious to enter into dialogue and discussions with Anglicans, realising that, behind our differences, we have much in common. . . . The problem as I see it has nothing to do with subjection or submission. The ultimate position of the Pope in relation to other bishops would depend upon Christian unity, and what sort of Church emerged out of the prayers and labours of Christian people. There is no question here of the Roman Catholic Church absorbing all other Christian Churches, but of the whole Christian world trying to rediscover and restore the one Church which Christ founded and which in the course of time has become split up through man's sin and folly.

In several recent sermons delivered on the west coast, moreover, Bishop Kilmer Myers of California had strong words to say on the same subject: [21]

What I therefore wish to say — for your further

147

reflection — is that we Anglican and Protestant Christians ought to reexamine our relationship to the Holy See as the chief spokesman for the Christian community in the world. In doing this I am not suggesting that in any sense we abjectly crawl to the feet of the Pope to ask his forgiveness and acceptance. The Second Vatican Council and indeed Pope Paul have pointed to the division of blame among all Christian communities for the present disunity of the Church. The Roman Catholic Church clearly is accepting its own share of the guilt of disunity. But, brethren, we must acknowledge our own guilt as well and this we have been somewhat less than willing to do. If Rome attempts to renew herself in full view of the whole world nothing less is required of us. . . . And we must admit our share in initiating and perpetuating the schism of the 16th Century. . . . If the Pope will undertake Christian amplification of his own real image we Anglicans and Protestants should consider most prayerfully our relationship to him. We should, I for one believe, acknowledge him as the Chief Pastor of the Christian Family and we should joyfully acclaim him as the Holy Father in God of the Universal Church. Such a move on our part, taken now, is far more important than our current consultation on the reunion of several American denominations. The truth is, we need the Pope because in this perilous age we need some one symbolically potent bishop to give expression to the Word of the Lord for our day. We need someone to say, as chief pastor in Christ, that the world-wide community of Christians must exert its massive power to halt war and conflict in the world. We need a chief pastor who will lead us in the fight against poverty and the powerlessness of peoples in the earth. *We need a Holy Father.* We need a Father who can speak and witness to the whole human race in such words as those contained in John's *Pacem in terris* or Paul's *The Progress of Peoples* and, quite simply, as the presence among us of the Fisherman. . . . We today may no longer even think of the reunion of Christendom without the Papacy. For a long time we have harbored the illusion that reunion would come by first uniting Anglicans, Protestants, and the Orthodox. Pope John has changed all of this . . . changed it all, I believe, by his faithful listening to the winds of the Holy Spirit. Our response to his response should be to seek ways by which spiritually (if not organically) we may return to a Papacy renewed and reformed. This, in my judgment, would in no way constitute a denial of our Reformation loyalties for Rome herself (including the Papacy) has accepted the principle of continued reformation in the Church.

And more recently still (January 1972), Archbishop Ramsey at Graymoor reiterated with new urgency the view that seems to have been his consistent stand ever since 1936:

It seems to me entirely acceptable that the spirit of truth reigns in the Church, and that when the Church collectively is guided into a common mind, it is for the Pope, as the presiding genius, to declare what that mind is.[22]

149

At the most official level, finally, is the Lambeth Conference whose decisions, although not binding, do carry great weight and persuasive force for Anglicans. The (latest) 1968 Conference moved slightly beyond previous ones in making these very balanced but friendly remarks in its final statement on the papacy: [23]

> As a result of the emphasis placed on collegiality at the second Vatican Council, the status of bishops in the Roman Catholic Church was in great measure enhanced though the teaching of the first Vatican Council on the infallibility and immediate and universal jurisdiction of the Pope was unaffected. We are unable to accept this teaching as it is commonly understood today. The relationships between the Pope and the episcopal college, of which he is a member, are, however, still being clarified, and are subject to development. We recall the statement made in the Lambeth Conference of 1908, and repeated in 1920 and 1930, 'that there can be no fulfilment of the Divine purpose in any scheme of reunion which does not ultimately include the great Latin Church of the West, with which our history has been so closely associated in the past, and to which we are still bound by many ties of common faith and tradition.' We recognize the Papacy as an historic reality whose developing role requires deep reflection and joint study by all concerned for the unity of the whole Body of Christ.

It has been suggested that this statement might have been even stronger had not the papal encyclical *Humanae Vitae* appeared on 29 July 1968 at the time of the debate.[24] Whether or not this is so, it is certainly true

that the first draft of the Lambeth statement was even
more positive in its gestures towards the papal see:

> The papacy is an historic reality whose claims
> must be carefully weighed in any scheme for the
> reunion of Christendom. Within the whole college
> of bishops and in ecumenical councils it is evident
> that there must be a president whose office in-
> volves a personal concern for the affairs of the
> whole Church. This president might most fitting-
> ly be the occupant of the historic see of Rome. Al-
> though as we understand them at present we are
> unable to accept the claims of the papacy to in-
> fallibility and immediate and universal jurisdic-
> tion, we believe that a considerable majority of
> Anglicans would be prepared to accept the Pope
> as having a primacy of love, implying both honour
> and service, in a renewed and reunited Church as
> would seem right on both historical and prag-
> matic grounds.

From all of the above evidence, therefore, I want to
suggest that the Anglican stance towards the papacy
since the sixteenth century has evolved from that of
"anti-papal" to one which today may at least be called
"non-papal." No exhaustive historical study of this evolution exists, and of course there is no statistical or
numerical proof; but I do think the above quotations indicate a contemporary Anglican attitude of openness,
of genuine interest, and at times of even more than mere
neutrality.

(2) Roman Catholic Views

Recent Roman Catholic discussion on the papacy has
been much stimulated, to say the least, by Hans Küng's

Infallible? An Inquiry (1971). Here our purpose will be to survey some of the current spectrum of views, and to observe that Küng's work has caused the contemporary Roman Catholic discussion to center almost exclusively on the doctrine of infallibility rather than on the wider question for ecumenical discussion of the total meaning of the petrine office in the Roman Church today. It has been well said, and I think indicated in the first part of this paper, that many Anglicans,[25] certainly the Old Catholics,[26] and possibly even the Orthodox,[27] would be willing to consider some rather flexible and limited sort of papal leadership for the entire church that would not be inconsistent with scriptural and patristic models and with the general sort of primacy acknowledged to the papacy during the first ten or eleven centuries of the church's history up to the age of the Gregorian Reforms.[28] But since 1870, and especially today, the discussion rages over infallibility,[29] and we need to survey some of the contemporary interpretations of it — both from historical and theological perspectives — before proceeding to an ecumenical evaluation for the future.

First on our list is an argument which has been raging for several years prior to Küng's recent book, primarily among historians and historical theologians of the conciliar period,[30] to the effect that the strict statements of infallibility defined by Vatican I and affirmed (in wider context) by Vatican II are in fact in direct conflict with the theory of conciliar supremacy over the pope in matters of faith, schism, and reform defined in 1415 by the Ecumenical Council of Constance in its decree *Haec Sancta*, a theory which was neither as recent in its origins nor as revolutionary in its claims nor as rapid in its demise as has been previously thought. There are many

shades of interpretation on this question, but for our purposes it will be sufficient to summarize by observing that
several reputable contemporary Roman Catholic scholars regard *Haec Sancta*, thus interpreted, as still dog-
matically valid and binding today.[31] In this view there
seems to be an irreconcilable conflict between binding
theories of conciliar and papal supremacy within the
Roman Church.

More recently, first in an article which appeared in the
Fall, 1971 issue of the *Journal of Ecumenical Studies*
and now in a book entitled *Origins of Papal Infallibility
1150-1350*,[32] the well-known Roman Catholic lay historian and professor of medieval history at Cornell University Brian Tierney has demonstrated convincingly that
the doctrine of papal infallibility had its origins in the
attempt of the Spiritual Franciscan Pietro Olivi in the
late thirteenth century to ensure the irreformability of
his interpretation of the doctrine of absolute poverty as
defined by Nicholas III in the bull *Exiit qui seminat* of
1279 against any possible alteration by papal successors.
In spite of the quashing of Olivi's attempts in the bulls
Ad Conditorem, Cum inter nonnullos, and *Quia quorun-
dam* of John XXII in the early fourteenth century, the
infallibility theory continued to be pressed by Ockham
and others as a safeguard against the doctrine of rather
unlimited papal sovereignty that had been the common
teaching of the canonists at the time of *Exiit qui seminat*. Thus, Tierney concludes, the doctrine of papal infallibility is something invented at the end of the thirteenth century for the purpose of restricting rather than
enhancing the power of the pope, it did not form any
part of the theological or canonical tradition of the
church before the thirteenth century, and today it has

the unfortunate effect of binding popes to decisions of their predecessors which they might wish to repeal. Tierney, whose credentials as an historian no one can gainsay, has produced an historical analysis which is unlikely to be faulted[33] and will certainly contribute to the current debate over the dogma of 1870. He has not, however, solved the problem of dogmatic development for the theologian nor has he given (or intended to give) any explanation of the positive meaning that belief in infallibility has had and does have in the lives and faith of millions of Roman Catholics.

So far we have considered some recent views of Roman Catholics who are primarily historians or historical theologians. When we turn to the more theological interpretations there seems to prevail a variety of *sitz-im-leben* approaches which all employ varying hermeneutical principles and qualifications or restrictions in order to produce evaluations of the papacy today that can in some sense be described as continuous with the 1870 definition.[34]

The first of these to consider is Küng himself, whose fundamental thesis — as has been observed — is by no means easy to determine.[35] To me, he seems to be denying the possibility of infallible propositions and to be opting for some doctrine like the "indefectibility" of the church, its perpetual abiding in the truth, a concept indeed popular with many Anglicans.[36] Rahner, it would seem, has criticized Küng for venturing outside the Roman Catholic theological community because he has chosen to demand "proof" of the infallibility doctrine in scripture and tradition rather than to accept it as the church's faith and then reason on the basis of it. Up to this date Küng still remains a priest and theologian of the Roman Church in good standing, and it is perhaps the way in which he is now treated — moreso than the substance of what he has said — that is of importance to Anglicans as they watch and try to assess the variety of teaching about the papacy that is in fact permitted within the Roman Church today. The view of Küng on the papal office most appealing to Anglicans is likely to remain his description in *The Church* of "a pastoral primacy of the Petrine ministry as the supreme court of appeal, mediating and settling disputes between the Churches."[37]

In the wake of the discussion on Küng, John McKenzie and Avery Dulles have given views of the papacy that are noteworthy for their positive testimony. McKenzie, who teaches theology at De Paul University in Chicago, says:

> Infallibility means at least this: The church and only the church knows what it believes, just as only I know what I believe. The church may not at this moment see its own mind clearly, as I may not see mine; it may not find the right expression for what it believes, it may find a better expression later, it may learn something which illuminates the dark corners of its faith. But ultimately if I wish to know what I must believe only the church can tell me what it believes. . . . I said the church; and therefore I think that *ex cathedra* must be clearly understood to mean that the pope speaks only *in* the church, never *to* the church. It must be the faith of the church and not his own which he proclaims if he is to speak with authority.[38]

And Dulles, the Woodstock Jesuit, comments:

Going somewhat beyond Küng, I should like to suggest that the Church, by reason of the promised assistance of the Holy Spirit, has a guaranteed power to adhere to God's truth in the face of heretical denials. Its infallibility is primarily negative: an assurance that it will not forsake the gospel. But the Church may on occasion receive the grace to speak positively, giving authoritative expression to what the gospel means in a particular situation. Such dogmatic declarations are attributable to the promised assistance of the Spirit of truth. When speaking in response to a threat to its existence as the herald of the gospel, the Church can speak, in a certain sense, infallibly.[39]

In other places Dulles has emphasized that infallible statements may not be easily distinguishable from fallible ones, and that they may be time-conditioned and in principle subject to revision.[40] And a similar sentiment has been noted by Bishop B. C. Butler: "Thus, paradoxically enough, one believes that dogmatic definitions are irreformable, and at the same time may hope that the doctrines they express may find expression in *new* formulations which will be verbally different from the original definition."[41]

Certain other contemporary Roman Catholic opinions should be cited. Professor Gustave Thils of Louvain (in 1969) is reported as writing that the Vatican I definition of 1870 was meant only to deny the *absolute* necessity of the church's formal approval, and that the relative (not absolute) assent of the church is still the habitual (not *sine qua non*) condition of infallibility.[42] Gregory Baum of Toronto (in 1968) is quoted of this opinion: "Infallibility means that, thanks to the scriptures and the living Spirit present in the Church, she is able to discern the meaning of God's Word addressed to her in the present and proclaim the revelation, once for all given in Christ, as the Good News for the contemporary world."[43] George Tavard, a member of ARC and ARCIC, writes (in 1968), "The task of the pope as first bishop in the apostolic college is to make collegiality visible. In his definitions, encyclicals, instructions, and actions he must embody the Church's unanimity, which is not reached by obedience to one man's opinions and decisions but by free and mutual consultation and discussion in the spirit of the Gospel. Papal encyclicals which do not embody this unanimity are theological documents with no claim on the allegiance of the Church's members."[44] And George Wilson, a Woodstock Jesuit, (in 1970) views infallibility as "the process by which the Church makes its way from the original data of faith to the contemporary formulation . . . . the mystery of God's power to use fallible instruments, and while respecting the laws of their human functioning to achieve unfailingly His own Self-communication."[45]

A more radical break has been advocated recently by the Roman Catholic ecumenical scholar Leonard Swidler[46] who prefers to emphasize "the discontinuity, the historicity" of supposedly infallible papal statements. After citing from past history many such examples of fully authoritative papal definitions and condemnations that have been "*reversed* rather than *developed*," he concludes:

> It must then be asked of the proponents of infallibility why the guidance of the Church by the Spirit has to be described in terms of the Church's

being prevented from ever embracing propositional error? Why could the Church not be described
as being guided in such a way by the Holy Spirit
that, if it did err, it would be capable of righting
itself, of renewing itself — just as God's Chosen
People of Israel did under the Spirit's guidance?
This constantly being recalled to the path of
righteousness and truth by the promptings of the
Spirit through prophesy and the "signs of the
times," by the constant study of the Scriptures
and Tradition would provide the essential elements of continuity and the avoidance of a complete relativism. To be sure, this approach also
contains difficulties and uncertainties, but does it
not seem to match better the historical realities
of man's life, which is full of difficulties and uncertainties?

What may we say, now, from all these contemporary
Roman Catholic views on papal infallibility? I think certain conclusions may be drawn. The medieval historians
who have studied the backgrounds of *Haec Sancta* and
Exiit qui seminat, as well as some few scholars like Küng
and Swidler, seem to prefer an out-and-out renouncing
of "infallibility" in favor of some concept such as "conciliarism" or "indefectibility." Most of the theologians,
on the other hand, seem to prefer retaining the term and
even the concept of infallibility in some sense, assigning
it a proper place in the history of dogma and then re-
interpreting it with various qualifications to mean what
they each think it should mean today. Although there is
not evidence to hand, I think that the hierarchy of Roman Catholic bishops, who are charged with teaching
the faith, would by-and-large also side with this latter

preference. Now it would be possible for me, as a medieval historian myself and as an Anglican, to agree with the former group in denouncing continuity only for continuity's sake and in concluding that the very concept of infallibility has died the death of a thousand qualifications in the attempt to make it meaningful today. Indeed, for an outsider it is difficult to avoid the Scotist *potuit, decuit, ergo fecit* observation that the only possible justification for it lies in the conviction that God could, and should have, and therefore did establish it in spite of the lack of evidence for it.[47] But for reasons that will be obvious in the last part of this paper, I prefer to conclude that the meaning and place of the term and concept of infallibility is largely a matter for dispute *among* Roman Catholics, within their own typology of the church,[48] which they must settle eventually in their own way. In the meantime, I think the dispute will continue to have interest among Anglicans for other reasons. First, it will be an indication of the limits of belief, of the possibility of doctrinal pluralism,[49] to be tolerated on this question within our great sister communion. And second, although at present (especially since Küng's latest book) this debate is concentrated rather narrowly upon the infallibility question, the discussion has behind it the much larger issue of the total meaning and value of the petrine office as a gift of God to the whole church, concentrated today most notably in the Roman communion's understanding of the papacy.

(3) Facing the Future in Dialogue

As both Anglicans and Roman Catholics look at the papal office in tomorrow's church, certain contours can be sketched. Anglicans generally will view the Roman see from at least a "non-papal," or neutral, stance, and many Anglican leaders will have even positive things to say about the possibility of some form of papal leadership in the church of the future. This approach will be based not only on a re-evaluation of the more significant role that the papacy is now acknowledged to have had in the New Testament and patristic periods as well as in the pre-reformation English Church, but also from a greater appreciation of what the papal office has meant in recent history. Thanks to the initiatives of Pope John XXIII and the Second Vatican Council, it is now impossible to conceive of the ecumenical movement, of the one church of Christ, of any serious Anglican plan for reunion, apart from some form of papal presidency in partnership with the church of Rome.

And from the Roman Catholic side, it is evident that doctrinal pluralism on the meaning of the papal office is now a live reality, and that many Roman Catholic theologians are describing it in ways that are less unacceptable to Anglicans. Vatican II began by placing the teaching on infallibility in the broader context of episcopal collegiality,[50] and still wider horizons seem probable as it is seen in relation to the doctrines of God, Christ, and the church.

Anglicans and Roman Catholics, however, represent different types of the one church of Christ, and it is probable—and perhaps even commendable—that they never will come to a precise common verbal agreement on the dogma of infallibility.[51] Although more thought and research is needed on the question, this dogma (as well as the direct papal intervention in minor local affairs) would seem to be a peculiar possession of the Roman communion, the particular way in which the petrine or papal office has been expressed within that tradition. Anglicans must have their own way of expressing this, their own typology of the papal office, and they must grapple seriously with the new evidence both historical and experiential. The polemics of the past have prevented a worthy Anglican expression of what this office might be, and very tentative statements have only just begun to emerge. The American continent, where the past controversies of the Reformation are not felt so deeply, seems a particularly promising place for this development. Anglicans must look seriously at the recent Roman Catholic experience of papal leadership in such fields as the Second Vatican Council, liturgical renewal, missionary strategy, and dialogue with non-Christians and the Third World. And, without getting side-tracked in the infallibility debate, they must ask their Roman Catholic brethren what the total papal experience has meant to them. The Roman Catholics, for their part, must try to answer not solely in terms of the old propositions but in terms that will be true to the contemporary doctrinal pluralism and to the possibilities of corporate reunion now posited by Vatican II in addition to the older tradition of individual conversions.[52]

If the Roman and Anglican communions look beyond their past polemics and propositional statements to the experiences they share even implicitly, they will find, I believe, that in fact they already do share a certain understanding of the pope as strengthener of the faith, as chief pastor of the Christian family, as personal embodiment of the truly catholic mission of the church universal. The statements they have inherited from the past certainly do not say all this; but their emerging theologies of Eucharist and ministry imply it, and their experience in many places is beginning to embody it.

There will be no seeking to lessen the legitimate prestige and the worthy patrimony of piety and usage proper to the Anglican Church when the Roman Catholic Church — this humble "Servant of the servants of God" — is able to embrace her ever beloved sister in the one authentic Communion of the family of Christ: a communion of origin and of faith, a communion of priesthood and rule, a communion of the saints in the freedom and love of the spirit of Jesus.

— Statement of Paul VI at the canonization of the Forty English Martyrs, 25 October 1970.

VI

REGIONAL UNION

A Theological Approach

by

WILLIAM F. MURPHY

SUMMARY

The possibility of a regional union of two dioceses, Roman and Anglican, must begin with a renewed theology of the local Church. Support for such a theology can be found in the early fathers, in Vatican Council II, and in many recent theological writings. Of particular importance is the concept of the Church as mission, which endows the mark of apostolicity with a dynamic thrust. Regional union can thus be possible for the sake of mission, provided that such basic preliminary conditions as agreement in faith, consensus on hard questions, and avoidance of scandal are met in advance.

In this paper we shall reflect theologically on the possibility of a regional union between two dioceses, Anglican and Roman. This union would be full, corporate and essentially sacramental. It would form one visible Christian community in one Lord, one faith, one baptism, gathered around the one table of the Lord.

Such a proposal obviously could be investigated from a variety of angles. There are demographic and sociological questions. There is the question of psychological and emotional preparedness. The relation of such a community to its neighbors not so united must also play a part.

This paper will not handle any of these questions. What follows will be an attempt to look at the proposal from a theological viewpoint, indeed from the viewpoint of Roman Catholic theological tradition.

Our basic question is this: What Christian traditions or theological developments are available to the Roman Catholic theologian so that he can describe the possibilities for positive action leading to such a regional union? What theological themes are there which would not deny or destroy the unity of Roman Catholics or the collegiality of their episcopate united with Rome but which would also allow, even urge a local or regional union with an Anglican diocese or group of dioceses to be accepted and sanctioned at this time?

This possibility will be examined in three parts. First there will be a consideration of the notion of the Church, what constitutes it and where it can be identified. Second, there is explored the implications of a mark of the Church, its apostolicity and the expression of its apostolicity in mission. Finally, some attempt must be made to apply these first two considerations to the present possibility before us.

I.

The post-Tridentine development of Roman Catholic ecclesiology almost without exception begins and deals exclusively with a theology of Church seen in its univeersal aspect. Thus Robert Bellarmine in his *De Ecclesia Militante*[1] makes no reference to the local Church. In his *De Summo Pontifice* and *Brevis Apologia*[2] he even excludes consideration of the local Church. The so-called "Roman School" of theology continued in this vein: the works of G. Perrone, C. Passaglia, J. B. Franzelin, L.

164

Billot and M. d'Herbigny do not develop any specific theological consideration of the meaning of the local Church.[3]

If, however, we return to the writings of the early Church fathers, different emphases emerge. Time and again the fathers explain the meaning of membership in the Church in terms of the local Church gathered around its bishop. For Ignatius of Antioch the Church is a unity or *henosis*, gathered about a single bishop. Spiritual unity of the Christian in Christ is conditioned by visible union with his representative, the bishop of this Church. With no prejudice to the collective episcopate, Ignatius can speak of a college of presbyters united about one bishop.[4] Similarly Eusebius of Caesarea sees the bishop as the throne in which Christ sits.[5] Origen, Irenæus, the *Apostolic Tradition* of Hippolytus, and Tertullian describe the functions of a bishop as keeper and preserver of a (local) Church. Cyprian in particular develops the notion of a fraternity of bishops within the Church. The function of each bishop then, is to care for his own Church, a function he exercises at the same time that he shares in the episcopal college.[6] We can conclude that the early fathers saw the local Church gathered around its bishop in much the same way that St. Paul earlier wrote to "the Church at Corinth" and in the same way that *Ekklesia* is used some 27 times in *The Acts* as referring always to local Churches.

Focussing again on our own times, we turn to the interesting and profound developments for faith and theology coming from the Second Vatican Council,[7] the fruit of much earlier theological reflection. The essays of J. Colson, Y. Congar, J. Ratzinger and, before them, of men like J. A. Mohler, had developed a richer and more nuanced theology of Church, a theology that allowed for new ecclesiological models to complement the prevalent "Roman School" model.[8]

Let us also look more closely at the statements of Vatican II. Chronologically its first contribution is in the Constitution on the Liturgy. In section 41 we read, "The bishop is to be considered the high priest of his flock. In a certain sense it is from him that the faithful who are under his care derive and maintain their life in Christ. Therefore all should hold in very high esteem the liturgical life of the diocese which centers around the bishop, especially in his cathedral church. Let them be persuaded that the Church reveals herself most clearly when a full complement of God's holy people, united in prayer and in a common liturgical service (especially the Eucharist), exercise a thorough and active participation at the very altar where the bishop presides in the company of his priests and other assistants."[9]

What is implicit about the local Church (diocese) in this description of the ideal of liturgical worship is developed even more clearly in two further council documents and one post-conciliar decree. The foundation stone is the perspective provided by chapter 2 of the Constitution on the Church. The prominence in this chapter of the People of God places the emphasis of ecclesiology strongly on the mystery of the Church, on the dynamism of that mystery and on the growing fullness of the Spirit that is realized in Christian community. The one People of God are in communion with each other. Diversity is not only to be expected but can be a positive stimulus. In section 13 we read, "Moreover, within the Church particular Churches hold a rightful place. These Churches retain their own traditions with-

166

out in any way lessening the primacy of the Chair of Peter." [10]

The subsequent concerns of the Church Constitution are influenced by this same perspective. So in Chapter 3, the description of the hierarchy is placed within the context of the notion of the People of God. Here sections 23, 26 and 27 time and again speak of the local Church in its function as a Church.

"This collegial union is apparent also in the mutual relations of the individual bishops with particular Churches and with the universal Church" (Section 23). "This Church of Christ is truly present in all legitimate local congregations of the faithful which, united with their pastors, are themselves called churches in the New Testament" (Section 26). "Bishops govern the particular churches entrusted to them as the vicars and ambassadors of Christ. . . . The pastoral office or the habitual and daily care of their sheep is entrusted to them completely. Nor are they to be regarded as vicars of the Roman Pontiff, for they exercise an authority which is proper to them, and are quite correctly called "prelates," heads of the people whom they govern" (Section 27). [11]

The functional unity of the local Church is also quite explicit in the Decree on the Bishops' Pastoral Office, *Christus Dominus*. Throughout this decree are found references to the local Church and to the manner of its function under the leadership of its bishop. Sections 3, 6, 11, 12, 17 and 36 in particular refer to the local Church, both in its relation to other Churches, especially the Church of Rome, and in its apostolic call to carry on the work of Christ and his Church. To quote just one section:

A diocese is that portion of God's people which is

entrusted to a bishop to be shepherded by him with the cooperation of the presbytery. Adhering thus to its pastor and gathered together by him in the Holy Spirit through the gospel and the Eucharist, this portion constitutes a particular church in which the one, holy, catholic, and apostolic Church of Christ is truly present and operative.

The individual bishops, to each of whom the care of a particular church has been entrusted, are, under the authority of the Supreme Pontiff, the proper, ordinary, and immediate pastors of these churches. They feed their sheep in the name of the Lord, and exercise in their regard the office of teaching, sanctifying, and governing. Yet they should acknowledge the rights which lawfully belong to patriarchs and other hierarchical authorities.[12]

A letter from the Sacred Congregation of Rites, issued 13 April 1967 and entitled *Eucharisticum Mysterium*, addresses itself to the role of the Eucharist in Christian life. In definite terms and with reference to section 26 of the Church Constitution (quoted above), this letter continues the view of the local Church as being a full Church in eucharistic unity gathered about its bishop.[13]

What then are our first conclusions? Without denying or attempting to diminish the primacy of the bishop of Rome or the unity that he ensures,[14] it does seem clear that, as the bishop receives his office from the mandate of Christ and as that office and the Eucharist are the guarantors of the ecclesial life of the people, the mystery of the Church is incarnate in the local Church (diocese) and the local Church, faithful to the gift of the Spirit,

has within itself a wholeness or completeness that reflects the totality of Church as the mystery of Christ's
love in truth.[15]

This expression of the mystery reflects the writings of
the early fathers. It has surfaced in more explicit terms
in the renewal of ecclesiology in the present century. It is
endorsed as legitimate in at least three constitutions and
decrees of Vatican II and is operative as a valid criterion
of the Church both in official documents (cf. *Eucharisticum Mysterium*) and in the continued reflection of the
theologians.[16]

II.

The promise of the Lord to be with his people has
never been accepted by the Church as a guarantee that
his will is already accomplished. Rather, as the Synop-
tics suggest, the promise of the Lord's presence is to
strengthen us to go forth, to preach the good news, and
to carry the Word to all parts of the earth.

It is this that animated the first disciples to travel the
Mediterranean world to gather all men in Christ. It is
this that earned these men the title of apostle. Basic to
all interpretations of this title is the notion of a mission
from Christ.[17] By preaching the Gospel, these men fulfill the will of Christ and authoritatively continue his
work which bestows on men the Spirit of God.[18]

Such a notion of apostolicity and mission ultimately
finds its basis in the Trinitarian mystery. For the mission of the Son from the Father and of the Spirit from
Father and Son offers us the paradigm of Christian life.
If the incarnation expresses the mission of the Son, surely then its implications (especially in terms of the call
to witness to the kingdom) must be continued in the in-

carnate Church animated and guided by the mission of the Spirit. Thus the apostolic Church bears witness to the meaning of the reign of God at this time and in this place.

Unity of faith and eucharistic communion are the springboard from which all Christian living arises. Their relationship to the Church's apostolicity and mission has been amply developed by M. J. LeGuillou: "The Church is not so much a gift as a promise. The visible unity of the Church is not given at the outset of missionary activity but at its term: it comes about as the response of God to the fidelity of the Church. We are then face to face with an ecclesiology of a Church in development, with a rationale of spiritual communion in development, with an ever greater visibility to the extent that there is fidelity to the Spirit as well as service to the mission."[19]

These themes are all interrelated: mission, communion, tradition, development. In this context mission becomes the vital expression of faith and communion is the continuation of an inherited tradition adapted now to this or that historical situation. It sets the course and guides the way to a development that can be comprehended as apostolic. To quote LeGuillou, "Mission concerns everything which within the Church or without is not yet completed."[20]

Fundamentally mission or apostolicity is a theological concept. It stems directly from an understanding of the Trinitarian mission as passed on to the community of believers. It is tied intrinsically to faith and sacrament as the application in this place and time of what the commitment to faith and the eucharistic communion imply. Its effectiveness, then, in the long run rests upon the ability of the Church to find the appropriate means to make its witness effective and its common life fruitful. It is at this juncture, then, that we can begin to see the possibility of regional union.

III.

To speak of this possibility is not necessarily to make it real. For while it is true that the Church does not have a divine sociology which demands an eternal and immutable social structure, it is equally true that regional union involves far more than the integration of parishes or open communion between an Anglican and a Roman diocese. Indeed, there must be established a prior hierarchy of goals and values. Sharing a school plant, or joint social action, is rather different from a sharing of sacraments. Therefore, it is necessary for us to set forth as clearly as possible the basic preliminary conditions.

First, there must be substantial agreement in faith. This may include not only the joint affirmation of the great creeds but the construction of a creed that will incorporate what may not be sufficiently expressed in the ancient formulas.

Second, while theological schools and pluralism in theology are to be encouraged, there must be substantial theological consensus among us, especially on those questions that have long exacerbated wounds: papacy, ministry, apostolic succession, liturgical practices. The Windsor statement on the Eucharist is the paradigm for this.

Third, there must be no great practical, sociological or psychological barriers to union among the peoples to be affected by it. All too often professional "Churchmen" plunge ahead heedless of the attitudes, hopes and desires of the people they ostensibly serve.

Fourth, the union must take place in such a way that it does not jeopardize the unity of the Anglican Communion from within nor the unity of the Roman diocese in the apostolic college under the headship of the Bishop of Rome. This, from the Roman side, would seem to demand the explicit recognition of this union as approved by the Bishop of Rome, a recognition which, again on the Roman side, would have to be explained publicly so that any seeming rupture in the college of bishops would be shown as non-existent.

These last four points have been negative and cautionary. Now we turn to the positive possibilities. If one grants all the guarantees just mentioned, and assumes a firm commitment to the Lord's Supper as the principal cause that fosters and nourishes our unity, it seems to this writer that a substantially good case for union can be made on the following grounds.

First, a greater realization of the meaning of the local Church arises. Gathered about the bishop, nourished by the Eucharist, faithful to the Word, it is Church.

Second, the Church must and now can seek more effective ways to make present the call of God's kingdom. This will demand that its witness be apostolic, a joint missionary activity to believer and non-believer alike.

Third, this witness will always be multiple and manifold. There are times when the universal Church must speak in clear terms about the universal faith as at Nicæa or Chalcedon. There are times when the visible sign of unity, the Bishop of Rome, must issue a call to all men as did Pope Paul at the United Nations in 1965. There are, however, many occasions, perhaps most moments in the life of the Church, when the witness is made not on a global scale but singly or in small groups.

These occasions, done in the context of a local Church union, are no less missionary, no less apostolic, no less the prophetic voicing of the Spirit by the Church of Christ.

What can be certain is this. Should a local Church find that, to be the witnessing Church, to be the prophetic sign to men, there is an apostolic mission to be performed which exceeds its own immediate resources, then there may be a call for the Anglican and Roman Communions to join efforts. Should the needs of this mission so demand, and should the basic preliminary conditions mentioned above be met, then those two local Churches under the leadership of their bishops may well be encouraged to strive for that regional union which will find Anglicans and Romans sharing at the eucharistic table so that they may together serve and extend their common apostolic mission.

The possibility rests on the intrinsic need of the common mission which in concrete terms will demand that these two dioceses act in the one Spirit that animates them both. It cannot be based solely on theological agreement, nor solely on pastoral, sociological or psychological desire. It *is* theologically based on the reality of the meaning of the local Church. But it is practically *realized* only if the theological notion of mission is made concrete in such a way that here and now the apostolicity of the Church of Christ demands that we so act and so live. May such a witness, in doing the mission that has called us together, be a witness leading the rest of Christ's Church closer to that final full communion for which we all pray.

173

A Planning Approach

by

RICHARD GARY

SUMMARY

There is a gap between the goals proposed by the international and national Anglican-Roman Catholic commissions and the present level of ecumenical practice at diocesan and parish levels. To bridge this gap, planning must occur and two factors ought to be present in it: (1) orderly organizational transition and (2) consistent involvement of the membership in the developing process of change. The possibilities of a plan of union and its implementation as stages of a process of growing together are assessed.

There is an enormous gap between the goals proposed by ARC and ARCIC and the present level of ecumenical practice at diocesan and parish levels. It is perhaps because of this gap that ecumenical discussion needs to be emphasized now in the diocese, not just in conversational form but in experiments as well. For ironically, the completed act of union will have to be concretized at the parish and diocesan level rather than the national. How this can be achieved in anything other than isolated exceptions will require a major concentration of attention and commitment. The discussion which follows is a planning approach to some of the implications of regional union. It will not attempt a systematic presentation of implementation phases, but rather highlight some possible approaches and present some examples of possible experimentation.

It would be a bit of an overstatement to suggest that ecumenical union has had to wait for the advent of the planning process, but as a resource no respectable institution should be without it. This essay will assume two nearly self evident concerns which we bring to any institutional union — *orderly organizational transition* and *consistent involvement of the membership in the developing process of change.* Since the Roman Catholic and Episcopal Churches are among the most institutionalized in Christendom, any melding in structure will require a strategy of organizational change. At the same time, the membership must be involved in any emerging new inter-relationship which affects them directly. To accomplish this balancing act, trust, faith and concern must be present in large portions.

What are the possibilities of a "plan" for ecumenical union?

Our topic, "The possibilities of a regional union," will need two tracks — what's happening to the organization? and what's happening to our people? This approach provides the essential considerations of leadership and membership. There may, on occasion, be a conflict in this duality, but the tension thus created by conflicting points of view can be constructive if it clarifies the respective role and responsibilities of each. In any case, we cannot back off from the essential reality-testing of each aspect of our corporate life. Ecumenical union suggests Christian renewal if we are to include a review of organization, mission, ministry. Such a review is not itself a renewal, but rather an examination of mission priorities with a recommendation as to how existing resources can be utilized to respond to new priorities. One methodology to do this is planning. As a self-directed review procedure, planning is a first step toward self-renewal.

I. Planning as Common Sense Approach

We are all familiar with the usual steps in planning. It begins with the identification of the problem — which is then analyzed. Principal goals are proposed along with alternative courses of action to achieve one or more of the options. When one alternative action course is selected, a method of validation is projected by means of experimentation. If the test is successful, a provisional conclusion is then ready for general application. If it is unsuccessful, you start over. As a simple orderly method of sorting out our difficulties and then doing something about them, planning has been widely utilized in a number of church organizations. When its common sense approach is coupled with a commitment to full disclosure of facts and broadly based decision-making, then new life has a chance to emerge.

Will planning work in a church setting?

Although planning is now operating in many institutional settings, it has a particular relevance for membership organizations. When major changes are under consideration, membership participation is essential if the effort is to succeed. Failure to do this violates our own standard of voluntary commitment to the Christian community. That may sound presumptive but we are the original volunteer organization. There are, of course, logistical difficulties in attempting democratic decision-making on a large-scale basis: It is difficult even on a small-scale basis. These are not insuperable difficulties, and we are not a naive people when it comes to reasonable political processes. Representative structures can be devised which will retain openness and manageability. The greater problem is one of the inner resiliency and strength of our Christian fellowship. Can we develop a new cohesiveness in the presence of such widespread despair and fragmentation?

The element of risk is always present.

New life in the Church as well as new life elsewhere faces a high risk. Two factors will reduce the level of risk somewhat. First, if from the outset diversity in point of view is anticipated, then communication and mutual acceptance will be strengthened. Second, if the widest possible latitude for local interaction is projected, then the local agenda will provide a context for the larger issues. The interrelationship between the larger and local issues is primarily a matter of scale and immediate relevance. Hopefully any plan, in substance and process, can be scaled larger or smaller as needed. It follows then — if you skip a couple of spaces — that the possibility for regional union will then be directly proportionate to the possibilities of national union.

II. Developing a Planning Model

Do these ecumenical discussions lend themselves to a planning format? If one finds himself refusing the thesis of this paper, then the answer to the question is no.

It will be maintained herein that there is a kind of sequence in development in these conversations which suggests a planning possibility. The pattern of interchange between the Anglican and Roman Catholic parties has already taken shape in the ARCIC and the ARC consultations. These discussions produced initial recommendations for further development of theological definitions and a mutual pledge of intention. Regarding the latter point the principal assertion resulting from the

ARC meetings was the reiteration of the goal statement "full communion and organic union." The significance of this mutual commitment by the commission members is repeatedly emphasized. How would the initial discussions provide a basis for a planning model? The following are the specific steps that it might include:

(1) *Initial exploratory discussions* of areas of agreement and disagreement identified, a general readiness for ecumenical union tested. The preliminary recommendations of ARC indicate that the initial theological reflection is well underway. The questions raised at this level lead to the second level, which is discussion of issues in detail and in depth.

(2) *Extensive depth exploration* of areas of doctrinal disagreement to reach tentative agreements, or agreement to lay over for later consideration issues which cannot receive recommendation at this time. Other issues which must be resolved at another level would be referred. Recommendation would be forthcoming from this discussion to the parent bodies. Final agreement on matters of major complexity need not be resolved at this stage, but tentative agreements on matters that affect corporate interrelationships will be necessary in order to move to the next step.

(3) *Proposals for general discussion* and selective experimentation recommended to parent bodies by the Commission. If the proposed action-plan is accepted by the parent bodies, widespread dissemination of recommendations and possible experimentation would be approved. A provisional agreement to proceed on certain critical elements

of the plan of union would serve some notice that the effort is under real consideration by both churches. It is at this point that tentative agreements could be tested in the subdivisions of the churches. This would include the regional considerations which will be discussed later.

(4) *Development of policy* which identifies doctrinal agreement, areas of separate development, organizational commitment and coordinated strategy of implementation.

On the basis of Step 3 a progressive development of policy commitments would emerge. Not at the same time but as agreed upon, major outstanding issues would be resolved into working agreements which would supersede the earlier provisional or experimental agreements. A comprehensive strategy would be developed as the shape and timing of the agreements indicate.

(5) *Organizational structures adjusted* to make the plan operational. Step 5 would require the integration of the existing structure in order to achieve the initial goal of organic union. Some separate development might possibly continue but subject to careful justification for exception status. Resource re-allocation is inseparable from organizational re-alignment.

A planning model, of 5 or 50 steps, is a device created to facilitate change in a particular system. As such it is somewhat technical in structure and function. But it is its purpose that matters and it derives that purpose from the organization. How is that purpose indicated in the model itself? Perhaps this can be seen by identifying the human factors present in the above five steps:

(1) *Theological development.* Our churches are called to serve a badly shaken, fragmented society. There are those who question whether we have the will, the resources, and the competence to define an authentic religious purpose. We carry the burden of proof — are we being called to seek a higher obedience which will provide a new coherence for us and for human brotherhood?

(2) *Identifying our disagreements.* In candor and in charity we must face our separation. Reconciliation has never been purchased cheaply. If the Christian Community can be reconciled we will have a gift to share with others.

(3) *Plan of action.* In our divided state our own needs require so much attention that we are neither examples nor servants of others. If we can agree on certain urgent matters and proceed to work on them together, a witness of unity will have at least begun. It is time that new priorities displace existing old ones: old commitments do not yield readily.

(4) *Development of policy.* Good policy is good news. Hard won truths are to be shared within the Christian brotherhood. They are badges of courage that will inspire hope and uplift confidence that love will triumph. A suffering humanity requires no less.

(5) *Our goal.* Full communion and organic union. To be one in Spirit inspires us to be one in work and witness. To share one ministry, one baptism and one sacrament. No less an objective would be worthy of our hopes.

III. Implications for Regional Union

What is a region? Since both the Episcopal and Roman Catholic Churches are diocesan in unit organization and episcopal in leadership, the obvious defined region would be that of a diocese. Dioceses are in practical and canonical terms largely self-constituted. A diocese may also subdivide into vicariates and regions if it desires smaller area groupings.

What is the relationship of a region to the national joint commission (ARC)? It seems probable that dioceses would take their cues on ecumenical matters from this commission, particularly when the commission's recommendations receive full official status. National policy guidelines and planning models would be judged on their merit, as indeed they should be, by the regional level.

Present ecumenical interrelationships. Most dioceses have existing ecumenical commitments. This activity can be enlarged upon on an *ad hoc* experimental basis. Without violating any church canons considerable local initiative could be directed toward programs of mutual benefit. Such joint efforts as Youth Service projects, family counselling, child care and self-help programs for older people could be shared with one another without canonical conflict.

Even more important, there is a wide variety of community programs which need church sponsorship. Much of the existing good will derives from these community efforts in which churchmen find themselves involved together in a humanitarian effort. The efforts of such experiences ought not to remain unrecognized by the churches. Acting in concert, joint church action can have a substantial effect upon community problems —

and in so doing can recast much of our thinking about ourselves.

Are there staff responsibilities that can be shared between dioceses? There are obviously some necessary preliminary steps to the sharing of staff. Conferences and retreats could provide the first contact, as has been suggested in the ARC recommendations. The bishops of the dioceses are the first and essential parties to any plan to coordinate or share personnel. Once there is an executive commitment then those persons with the "leading edge" union responsibilities can be given clear signals to move ahead in developing the necessary research and planning, with follow-up functions in training and program not far behind.

The sharing of bishops should be a high agenda item in episcopal conversations. With dioceses decentralizing into regions and vicariates, new roles and functions for episcopal leadership are now an organizational possibility in the larger dioceses. The theological issues involved are being discussed elsewhere, but as a part of a plan of union when the bishops sit down to discuss the sharing of duties, the church and the world will know we are serious about ecumenical union.

Interdiocesan ecumenical commission. In order to underline the importance of the Anglican-Roman Catholic dialogue, Episcopal and their geographic counterpart Roman Catholic dioceses could form their own version of the ARC commission. Charged with responsibility to implement the recommendations of ARC, this interdiocesan body could then plan for and press for the application of these recommendations, as a third force group with direct access to the diocesan decision-making units. The interdiocesan commission would have the kind of freedom and initiative that seems to characterize the ARC group. A commission whose vocation it is to render an ecumenical witness could be an important factor in inducing union.

IV. EXPERIMENTATION — SOME POSSIBILITIES

In many urban areas Episcopal and Roman Catholic churches are not working together either at a diocesan or interparish level. Given the urgency of the inner city crisis a major ecumenical effort should be mounted without delay.

(1) *In the New York area.* The South Bronx can be considered as a possible focus for an ecumenical community project. It is a scene of desolation. Housing is urgently needed, rehabilitated or new. Health services are wretched, and the schools are in disarray. Suppose the Archdiocesan and the Diocesan leadership agreed to rally city, private and other church bodies in a major effort to help the community reclaim its life. Conceived as a major self-help project, the churches would serve as resources to community leadership. One of the resources in this effort might very well be the parochial schools, which, under joint church and community sponsorship, could find a new public role which would in turn attract public and private support. Community self-help, now under great duress, might become a reality if the people and the city realized the churches were going to stand together in this scene of desperate need. There is considerable indication that the Church can rally and spread participation if it will lead the way. Such a positive effort does not require

any major theological compromises; in truth just the opposite might be the case. We might be fatally compromised if we chose not to act.

(2) *Suburban city interchurch coalition.* Again in New York, the major suburban city areas are under enormous stress. They lack political stability. Potential leadership centers in business, industry and often political parties. A dangerous deterioration of public morale and general social purpose has ensued. Church interrelationships are often undeveloped — which fact contributes to the downward spiral rather than resists it. There exists in these areas a major opportunity for ecumenical initiative.

If an interchurch coalition proposed a series of initiatives in housing, community self-help programs and community interaction programs (to reduce intergroup tensions), other agencies and civic groups would sense a new alternative. Such cities are centers of sizable church membership constituencies. If we cannot speak effectively to our own, we may be rightly accused of abandoning them.

(3) *Small town ecumenical activity.* As in other community settings what is done in the small town must be self-initiated and appropriate to the local needs. Leadership roles are suggestive and supportive by intention.

In one small town the planning committee of an Episcopal congregation sought out its church neighbors to see what kind of a common life they might share. The results of their inquiry are revealing. They found an immediate interest in common youth programs, children's religious education, and direct service programs such as Day Care, Family Counselling and drug addiction treatment. Other institutional needs — such as a common church office center, central purchasing and shared maintenance were proposed. Uniform interest was indicated in an expanded Christian fellowship through common programs, issues of mutual interest, and occasional social gatherings. Combined worship services were not ignored, but were last on the list of interactions.

What about public issues on which we are known to disagree? There will undoubtedly continue to be matters of public policy on which we will have to agree to disagree. In some cases there may be an accommodation as conditions change. For example, on the matter of direct aid to parochial schools Episcopalians have tended to be discreetly quiet. We now might attempt a re-consideration that will find public acceptance. In other areas of frequent disagreement we will probably need an "out of bounds" category, which we will agree not to discuss till everything else is settled. The prime candidate for this category would be nearly all matters relating to human sexuality. Our widely divergent views on this vast subject could push us into a polarization that would undercut the strength of any new-found unity.

V. NEXT STEPS — ALL INITIATIVES NEEDED

Ecumenism is a movement of the Spirit before it is anything else. The union movement must be allowed and encouraged to move where it will. People, parishes and dioceses must be free to respond as they are inspired and guided to do so. It is the function of the institutions to host and strengthen this call to new life. We must remember that our traditional commitments are not inviolate standards — they are too often what was left behind when everything else moved on.

Clergy and laity should be encouraged to seek new relationships, new ways to witness and news ways of working with their brothers in the faith. If planning has a basic role, it is to keep the church system open to new initiatives for new life from whatever source.

The challenge has been thrown down by our leaders and by the convergence of urgent circumstances. In our communities there will be an endless variety of cooperative actions, ranging all the way from goodwill gestures to major coalitions. In our dioceses and parishes, we may be more conservative, moving as if our kinship in the church isn't quite as urgent as our brotherhood in the world. And maybe it isn't. The societal crises which threaten to engulf us may require all the energy we have. If our dialogue replenishes that energy, let it proceed forthwith; but if it is a comfortable distraction, it can wait until other fires abate.

It is, however, the underlying contention of this essay that action and reflection can proceed in tandem, not necessarily step by step, but in a recognized and hopefully planned interrelationship.

VII

SOCIOLOGICAL AND CULTURAL FACTORS

A Sociologist Looks at Ecumenism

by

Eugene J. Schallert, S.J.

SUMMARY

A Sociologist observing the phenomenon of ecumenism would be interested in the discovery of two different groups of people — those who have already achieved a degree of union and those who remain separate. He would assume that religious convictions have something to do with union and disunion but he would like to investigate the human correlates of these convictions. He knows that faith does not occur in a vacuum and that items of belief are associated with sociological, cultural, socio-psychological, economic and political facts. Do systems of belief unite or separate people or are these systems selected to legitimize existing unions or disunions?

Sociological research does little, if anything, by itself. Knowledge stored in a computer or on a library shelf is seldom used. Because Sociologists are aware of the significant contributions they have made to human development in the past, they are more concerned than ever that their discoveries be put to use. Important breakthroughs have been made in the implementation of research findings. Thus, Sociology, through both research and implementation, can contribute significantly to the process of growing together. In view of the widespread acceptance by both Churches of the value of Sociology for religious development, it would seem inopportune to ignore this potential in the present ecumenical efforts of the two Communions.

187

1. Goals and Perspectives

In 1964, Pope Paul VI, devoting the whole of his Christmas Message to the theme of brotherhood, showed his sentiments in action by declaring when on the point of leaving Bombay, that this pilgrimage, so unusual for a Pope, was conceived as "a voyage of peace and love to strengthen the bonds of mutual understanding and friendship between all peoples, reminding them of their binding duty to acquire knowledge of one another, to love one another and to help one another effectively according to the variety of gifts received from God."[1] In still stronger terms and directed to a particularized situation, Archbishop Ramsey, standing in the heartland of apartheid, condemned the deliberate policy of segregation in South Africa as being diametrically opposed to the Christian message of brotherhood.

Perhaps the detente is the result of approaching ecumenism on a front that is too broad and therefore filled with an over-abundance of insoluble problems for this point in history. For this reason a mutual study of the Roman Catholic Communion and the Anglican Communion seems opportune in that there are apparently large areas of common ground from which to begin. In these Communions there is the least amount of dilution and fragmentation that needs mending. This fact was noted in the Vatican II document on Ecumenism where it states: "Among those Communions in which some Catholic traditions and institutions continue to exist, the Anglican Communion occupies a special place."[2] It is for this reason that initial efforts have first opened with the Church of England on the theological plane. This also is the reason that we here direct our efforts to study the relationship that exists at another level between the Church of Rome and the Church of England.

As we move from the area of dogmas to that of concrete human relationships, we can see that the immediate brotherly community of believers is made up of communicants. Admittedly, the brotherhood that now exists between Roman Catholics and Anglicans includes the fact that both belong to different fraternal communities. It includes, too, the separation and the pain of this separation, and presents a constant challenge to overcome it. Though it is important not to ignore the element of separation which is an inevitable part of brotherhood and gives it its particular quality, nonetheless, to ignore it is ultimately to become reconciled to it. "Separated brethren," which has become such a glib phrase, can thus acquire an exact and valuable meaning. Can sociologists probe into this dimension of a common brotherhood? Is there an awareness or a consciousness of a community of believers which in some way or another transcends the consciousness of diversity or separation?

It is one of the hoped for results of a sociological study that eyes will be opened to those particular elements belonging to the preaching, the Church structure and practice of the other confession which might be missing in the preaching and practice of one's own church. It is also hoped that what will be achieved will embrace the riches of faith and life of both churches to the extent that they are in harmony with God's revelation and Christ's intention.

In this way the appreciation of the unity and communion that already exists will not tend to dilute or obscure things that are essential, but it will stimulate a deepening and widening process. The above, though frequently said in past years, deserves to be reiterated. Not only is it important to give visible signs of brotherhood but also to work toward the promotion of that brotherhood that is basic to the life of every single individual. This integration must not be imposed as a demand from above but must be the fruit of a process of maturation in which both churches are jointly involved. Though the doctrinal aspects of these questions should be continually studied by the theologians, this effort may be facilitated as the churches and their ministers grow in the direction of an awareness of common viewpoints regarding the function of religion and religious authority.

There is an observable sluggishness in the ecumenical movement. This has been partially the result of being distractedly absorbed in the theological dialogue and sometimes superficial fraternal fellowship. It is also partially the result of disregarding the living nexus that exists between communicants and their hierarchies, the people and their institutions. This nexus is the minister who infleshes the ideologies, the tenor of the times and of his Communion. It would seem that if ever the two Communions are to achieve formal union, it will be through the impact of their ministers.

Therefore the purpose and problem of a sociological study is eminently practical. This same concern presently being faced by Rome is the restructuring of a theology and practicum of the priesthood with an eye to the world at large and to those communities separated from the church.

The orientations evident in the Lambeth Conference of 1958 highlight two points that were previously mentioned: that the Anglican Communion, in dealing with a proposed rapproachment with the Presbyterians, relied heavily on a common understanding of the ordained ministry and that it was the fulcrum between the church and the faithful, and between the church and Christ.

William H. Van de Pol, addressing himself to the Anglican ecumenical effort, states:

> If the signs are not misleading, we stand at the beginning of a truly existential ecumenical dialogue between the Church of Rome and all other Churches, and not in the presence of a dialogue that is chained to a priori conditions and restrictions. In this encounter the problem of ministry, and in connection with it the question about the continuity of the Church, will ultimately take the central place in the dialogue. It is the important results obtained through the conversations, between the churches of the Anglican Communion and practically all other churches during the last twenty-five or fifty years, that will undoubtedly offer fruitful suggestions.

What Father Van de Pol seems to suggest is that at the heart of any future ecumenical effort is the understanding and restoration of the ministry in the Church in its existential context. This same note is struck by Augustin Cardinal Bea at a lecture delivered at Heythrop College, Oxford, August 7, 1962 when he invites the priests particularly to "consider with me those elements in our priestly calling which have a special bearing on efforts for unity."[3]

In his address Cardinal Bea placed stress on the areas of theology, philosophy and practical working relations. We are here concerned with a field of endeavor that is inclusive of all of this and attempts a synthesis at the level in which the priest lives and moves and reacts to each of these realities. Aside from a priest being "set apart" he is basically a social being who interacts with ideas, systems and people in the world around him. This fact did not escape the Fathers of Vatican II when they insisted in several citations that "appropriate use must be made not only of theological principles, but also of the findings of the secular sciences, especially of psychology and sociology."[4]

Both churches have sponsored joint endeavors to deal with pluriformity in philosophy and theology, in history and scripture. Joint ventures have taken place in worship and in particularized social concern, especially as these affect the problem areas of the Third World. What is intended in a sociological study is an attempt to discover these syntheses as they are reflected in the lives of the ministers who are the sacramental visible referent to the mysteries of the invisible God. In this regard, sociology is of singular value both in discovery of de facto systems of belief, their development and modification in the modern world, and in the many social factors which may or may not contribute to the ability of the minister to express himself and to relate to the needs of his people.

The visible unity of the two Churches cannot be the only objective, though certainly it is one of the penultimate goals. There must be a deeper understanding of what Pope John XXIII alluded to as an already existing "invisible unity" that comes from baptism, charity and from professing, at least partially, the same faith. This invisible unity must be understood not only in its theological framework, but in its sociological context.

Within this social dynamic, the priest has been the

nexus, and it is he who must be understood in this light. Whatever culminating results of history, philosophical thought, theology and religious institutions have been achieved, can best be understood in the context of priests reaching for unity. It is the priest who must be understood as the concrete referent before unity can take place, before the visible sign of the invisible God can become more manifest, before the Church can have a healing and elevating impact on the dignity of person . . . strengthen the seams of human society and enrich the everyday activity of men with a deeper meaning and importance . . . contribute toward making the family of man and its history more human.[5]

2. THE SOCIOLOGY OF ECUMENISM

Because of the recent advances in ecumenism in the area of theology, it seems most appropriate that an in-depth sociological investigation which is both ecumenical and international be undertaken to determine those de facto qualities which prove either unitive or divisive. It has been observed, for example, that Anglican and Roman Catholic priests exhibit somewhat ambivalent behavior, particularly when the social service areas of their parishes and/or apostolates overlap. In some locales, the priests from each Church work in considerable harmony while elsewhere they demonstrate great antipathy for each other. Further, it has been observed that those priests who, in fact, work in close harmony with each other, while maintaining their respective doctrinal convictions, seem less concerned with doctrinal or religious differences. On the other hand, those priests who are warring with each other or who are, at least, oblivious of each others' common commitment to scripture and Christian tradition, seem pre-occupied with these differences. Thus, it is suggested that certain identifiable barriers exist which artificially divide the two Churches. Defective communication seems to be one of these. It seems then that the basic human and spiritual qualities of the members of the two Churches are essentially compatible, but selective elements of their human and spiritual beliefs are utilized in a divisive way.

Is there any practical, ecumenical value to sociological research? Clearly, surveys of a purely demographic and content-free nature are of little but descriptive value. Decisions on any level cannot be made with this kind of information as a base. Though virtually mountains of information have been collected and carefully analyzed by sociologists of both the past and present, it does not follow that all sociologists devote their academic lives to the task of data collection and analysis. Today especially sociologists are concerned with implementation. Social studies, however, cannot change the world even when they are conducted in the more substantive areas of belief-systems, ultimate values and basic life-style patterns. Studies *have* been of significant and demonstrable help to individuals and groups in their efforts to solve the problems which confront them. For while research cannot give people strength, it can help them discover their existing and frequently latent resources.

The tragic separation which has occurred in the history of the churches has hardened not only into distinct mentalities and systems of belief, but also into different institutional and organizational structures. The scandal of disunity seems to have become institutionalized. There is a suspicion that the pervasive influence of such institutional factors is all the more powerful and resistant to change since they are mostly ignored and un-acknowledged. These institutions are the givens of separate religious life. Or are they? We know, in fact, that social structures and institutions both express a particular mentality and, in turn, contribute to moulding that mentality. It is inevitable, therefore, that socio-cultural systems have an influence on religious thought, and it is an understanding of this that will provide another key in opening the door for eventual unity.

Leadership in the direction of ecumenism has been given. Has this direction become an integral part of the institutional structure of the priesthood as this might be evidenced in the belief systems, the brotherhood or the life-style of the priests of both Communions? These areas have been generically central in the union/disunion of the Christian Churches. They should be looked at sociologically to uncover those specifics which, in fact, have contributed to separation or "growing together" of local Churches.

A sociologist would probably be concerned with some or all of the following areas in his investigation of union and disunion.

Belief

In undertaking a study of this type, it is assumed that ideas (cultures, meanings, belief items, etc.) have a measurable effect on pastoral-ecumenical orientations. Thus, a probe should be made for those propositions relating to faith and order, to Church and ministry, to authority and sacraments and to the manner in which these are associated with ecumenicity and its opposite. Which propositions are present when priests of the two Communions are one and which when they are apart?

Does the degree of affective involvement with these propositions effect union or separation? In the minds of the clergy of both Communions, what is the relationship between these unifying-separating propositions and the substance or base of their belief experience? Do those who are farthest apart use theological explanations as rationalizations for their own disunity?

Life-Style and Spirituality

Since faith does not exist in a vacuum nor exclusively in the minds of people, the sociologist would tend to investigate the correlates of Christian belief. For example, the life-style of the clergy in both its religious and secular dimensions can be presumed to have an effect on ecumenicity. Spirituality is also hypothetically associated with union or disunion. Assuming some integration of secular/religious life-style, on the one hand, and spirituality on the other (an assumption that would have to be tested), a research team would be concerned with the detection of either life-style patterns or spirituality which form barriers to or aid in the development of ecumenicity. For example, if the secular culture demands that clergymen work together on some common project, has this kind of union caused them to question their religious unity or disunity? Life-style is frequently subject to pressures to conform. Have these pressures been translated to anything deeper than external patterns of behavior?

Community Life and Communication

In this section an in-depth probe into the amounts and kinds of communication, both vertical and horizontal, should be made. The members of both Communions could be asked to reveal not only the frequency with which they communicate within their own denominational parameter and across denominational lines, but also the kinds of expectations they have relative to their own dialogic life against their own internalized aspirations and ideals. Do they converse with others as frequently and as deeply as they feel they should? Does the presence or absence of adequate communication contribute to differential expectations relative to growing together?

Community life is the most difficult phenomenon of all to investigate because there are so many aspirations in the direction of the Christian community and so little reality to examine. In order to understand, however, the depths of ecumenical endeavors, the orientaions of Anglicans and Roman Catholics toward Christian community or fellowship, toward brotherhood and reconciliation should be carefully examined. Do ecumenically minded pastors, for example, have a different hierarchy of values — life-style, brotherhood, service — from those who are not ecumenically inclined? Can the same be said of the laity? Where brotherhood is given primacy, is it limited to parochial parameters or does it transcend the barriers of likeness?

Authority and Freedom

Attitudes, opinions and evaluations of religious people on the whole question of authority and freedom are obviously immensely important with regard to ecumenism. Do both Anglicans and Roman Catholics express a need for authority? Are they satisfied with bureaucratic authority or do they sense a need for an authority which is more traditional or more charismatic? Is there too much administrative authority in their lives with a concomitant power vacuum in the goal-setting, integration, reconciliation and cultural dimensions of their own society? Do they view authority as too much preoccupied with its own "house-keeping" and insufficiently concerned with reconciliation and service? Is this true across denominational lines and will these authority problems effectively discriminate between ecumenically minded priests and those not so inclined?

Ministries: Traditional and Creative

Ministries are at least theoretically associated with needs. Most of the ministries of Anglican/Roman Catholic priests were creatively designed to meet the needs of existing populations. Since a sociological study would be initially concerned with the clergy of both Communions, it would be important for the investigators to "zero-in" on the priests' definitions for the needs of their communities. In the opinion of Anglican/Roman Catholic priests, what kinds of needs, latent or overt, are present in today's world? How do they read the "signs of the times"? Are their perceived needs different from those which existing ministeries were designed to meet? Are new ministries to be designed in terms of the Pauline charisms, in terms of the anthropologically generalized functions of religion or in terms of what has traditionally been referred to as the spiritual and corporal works of mercy? If, in the section on authority and freedom, the sociologist discovers that a credibility gap exists between clergy and hierarchy, he may discover this gap is associated with the absence of those ministries creatively designed to satisfy some of these unforeseen needs. If, in the section on belief systems, he discovers low affective

198

involvement with those propositions negatively associated with ecumenism, then he may also discover something about the specific design of these new ministries. If, in the section on dialogue and the Christian Community, he discovers low satisfaction with the parameters of both, then he also may find out how to restructure the symbol system and the organizational development of both Communions.

Social-Psychological Barriers to Ecumenism

There are many social-psychological factors which play an important role in inhibiting the "growing together" phenomenon. If such factors as alienation, authoritarianism (or an obsessive concern with power), problems associated with identity and maturity, etc., are not confronted and/or resolved, they will very likely become the sources of inertia and conflict in any movement toward unity. If these factors are operating in a dysfunctional way, then no matter how high dialogue and community rank in the priest's or layman's hierarchy of values, they will not be able to achieve the realization of these values, especially in an ecumenical way. It is important at the outset to identify those factors which are operative as barriers to ecumenism so that the two Communions can realistically ascertain the most successful methods for neutralizing and/or eliminating them.

Sociological Dimensions

Dissatisfaction, unhappiness, low morale are clearly associated with stress. The major strains measured by other researchers among the clergy are unmistakeably related to apprehension about the value of one's career or one's job in the service of the real needs of men. Clerics who have either painted themselves into a sacristy corner or have helped others to place them there find that, in the last analysis, they are both rejected by the laity and are personally and religiously alienated. Narrowly defined role conceptualizations are seldom productive of high career, job or personal satisfaction. Nor are such role definitions productive of ecumenical/pastoral orientations. Predictably, the "house-keepers" of the two Communions will not be the ecumenists.

It has been observed in the past that the members of the Anglican Church have tended to occupy different positions in society than members of the Roman Catholic Church. Their educational background was different, their socio-economic status was different and their ethnic composition was different. Many of these significant differences have virtually disappeared today, but the tendency to identify membership in the two Churches in terms of these differences has remained. The reality has changed; the image is the same. A sociologist, who is concerned with union or disunion, would like to know if these differences are based upon previous facts and present fictions or upon present realities.

Moral Orientations

There is also the very important moral dimension to take into consideration. How deeply does the Church, for example, through its ministers, enter into the private lives of its people? What kinds of expectations do priests think people have of the Church as a teacher of morality? Are propositions enough or do people expect more of their priests? Are there any detectable hierarchies of moral values within the working consciences of priests?

Where does their sense of "the moral" place ecumenism on their hierarchy of values? How do priests handle the morality of the "unprecedented situation"? If the "scandal" of a divided and frequently warring Christianity was not morally wrong in the past, has it become wrong in the present for those priests whose ecumenical/pastoral orientations are great?

Growing together is a complex phenomenon. It is more than a doctrine or a moral code. Certainly it is associated with the factors elucidated throughout this paper. The strategy involved in researching this "event" is to find those priests who are one, those who are becoming one and those who are not growing at all. Priests will have discovered that their pastoral orientations toward each other, toward the laity and toward the world are more alike than unlike. The laity, in turn, will have discovered their unity when they have discovered that their orientations toward their priests, their fellow laymen and the world are more alike than unlike.

3. CONCLUSION

Research cannot be successful when it is viewed as a substitute for action. Frequently, when individuals do not *want* to make a decision, they begin a study as a delaying tactic. But, when sociological studies are viewed as a tool to locate the precise area where action can be undertaken successfully, then they can be quite fruitful.

Research is successful when it is scholarly in terms of all the disciplines involved and when it is adequate to the complexities of the issues being probed. Far too many amateurish studies have already been done and far too many failures experienced.

Sociological studies are most valid when they attempt

to encompass more than one point in time or space. They must be longitudinal if they are to discover something more than ephemeral opinions, ideas or feelings determined by fads, passing fancies and so forth. The attitudes discovered through the instrumentality of sociological research are factual. They are not normative. They do reveal areas of human interaction wherein truly normative input is needed. The facts revealed in the studies tell us where we have succeeded and where we have failed in the transmission of Christian norms and consequently where we can best direct our own activity.

Since growing together is presumeed to be a process and since the sociologist is concerned with both research and implementation, the elements of this process will be fed back to groups under study in a precise way. In like fashion, the elements of the process of separation would be reported to both groups under study. Thus, research and implementation become one process which is integrated into the total process of growing together.

Studies which probe for human interaction in all of its complexities are far more successful than those which investigate ideological interaction and conflict. Some theoreticians feel that ideas and ideologies govern human behavior. Others, perhaps more realistically, believe that ideas, belief-systems, moral norms and so forth are but one of many factors present in human interaction or the lack thereof. In this context, it would be interesting to find out if the fellowship present in the Anglican/Roman Catholic International Commission (which has devoted itself to the discovery of a consensus in the areas of Anglican and Roman Catholic belief) is a function of the coming together of religious ideologies or the coming together of religious men.

If the study is successful, then the responsible members of the two Churches will know where to build and what therapies to apply. They will no longer be treating symptoms. They will also know where they have failed and where they have succeeded. As noted above, an ecumenical study should be longitudinal and international. Since it takes place across time and space, successes at one point in time or space can be implemented in other points and failures eliminated. In a sense, the study would become a continuous and scholarly monitoring device for the phenomenon of growing together.

At any point in the investigation/implementation process, policy decisions of a strategic nature could be suggested to the highest authorities of both Communions. If research in the Sociology of Religion can help individuals learn something of the mechanics or methodology of reconciliation, then, perhaps, these individuals can teach others how to bridge other chasms which separate the human family. The seriousness of the two Churches as they approach a self-study of this kind and its implementation will make their message of brotherhood more credible to men who are separated by racial, ethnic, national or other barriers.

Unifying Roman Catholic and Episcopal Parishes

by

GEORGE A. SHIPMAN

SUMMARY

How can the readiness of paired Roman Catholic and Episcopal parishes to live as unified Christian communities be tested? Here an experimental approach is suggested. By survey research and related methods, four critical attributes can be probed. Parish profiles can then be developed and analyzed. Methods of organization development may be useful for inducing needed attitudinal change.

The points of theological agreement reported among the membership of the Anglican-Roman Catholic International Commission (ARCIC) and of the counterpart commission in the United States (ARC) are of great significance. The apparent convergence is good news for Christians, and should be received with joy and gratitude, but with the recognition that there are other significant questions still unanswered. Some of them can be resolved through thoughtful study and consultation. But a different approach is indicated for one category of issues. These can be framed in the question: Are Roman Catholic and Episcopalian parishes in the United States ready to live as unified Christian communities?

This paper addresses itself to that question. The approach is not theological, and it does not purport to be a systematic sociological analysis. The point of view is rather that of an organization analyst, working from one situation to another, developing specific working designs geared to the apparent requirements of each situation. The only commitment is to the basic discipline of building an analytical model and testing it for operational utility. This experimental approach is used also in the hope it will stimulate others toward the refining of the conceptual framework, the design of testing instruments, and the projection of developmental strategies.

Very little is known about parish readiness for one or another degree of unification. This must be recognized at the outset. Such studies as are available — the work of Glock and Stark comes to mind — were not designed to deal with the specific question. The widespread application of findings of their major study, *Religion and Society in Tension*, would also be arguable, since four California counties were the research site. It seems reasonable to assume that broad generalizations do not apply. Some pairs of parishes may now be ready for some degree of unified community life. Others are not. The task, then, is how to approach and test the state of readiness in any specific situation.

For purposes of this exploration, the degree of coalescence of any two parishes is not tightly defined. Presumably it would be something more than sharing of facilities, but something less than unification within a mutually encompassing institutional framework as yet undefined. Perhaps what is involved is a growth process. Its first stage is more than a matter of facilities used in common, but less than institutional unification in the comprehensive sense. In these terms it can then be assumed that, while the two communions retain their institutional identities, the combined parish would incorporate the life of a unified Christian community interrelating within it the local projections of both communions. Such variables as property holdings are expressly excluded from consideration at this point. The focus is upon the essentially socio-cultural aspects of the Christian community that seem critical to its capacity to function as a means for Christian nurture and witness.

This path of analysis leads to three central questions. First, what major variables determine the degree of unity that can be realized in any particular parish-to-parish situation? Second, can the state of these variables be tested, and possibly measured, in the particular situation? Third, can blocks to unity, identified as such, be modified by inducing change? The first question is the primary concern of this paper. Unless it can be answered with confidence, and the answer supported with a convincing degree of validation, the other questions obviously cannot be considered in any depth. They will be touched upon only briefly here.

The Framework

Stated in brief, the idea of the Christian community used here is that of a collectivity of persons, individuals and families, which as a social entity:

1. Holds in common the essentials of the Christian belief system;
2. Is strongly motivated to express its beliefs in cooperative expressive action;
3. Has a generally accepted location in physical and social space, symbolized by a center, or centers, for worship, interaction, and cooperative expression;
4. Places a sufficient value upon its common life to supply economic support essential to continued productive existence.

These attributes are assumed to be essential to the realization of community, and thus each requires some further commentary.

1. The Belief System

It seems possible to assume that the sense of controlling societal ethics in the American scene is rooted in the Judaic-Christian traditon. This is a generalization, but one borne out by substantial evidence in the literature and in the observation of behavior. The existence of a civic ethic would be difficult to deny, however much or often its obligations are waived. Denominationalism or, more accurately, religious pluralism seems not to diffuse this basic ethical commitment. It underlies the generally accepted criteria for weighing the ethical values of alternative choices, and for appraising the outcomes of individual or group action.

This civic ethic is variously perceived and interpreted. But the variations seem unrelated to differences in denominational affiliation. The differences associated with religious pluralism as such appear to be in the ways ethical commitment is generated and refreshed through styles and modes of worship, methods of expression, variations in ecclesiastical polity, and the like. These differences relate more to inherited traditions, cultural and national, and to accumulated life styles, than to the substance of the ethical commitment.

The central attributes of the Christian commitment are not for exploration here. But it may be suggested that the Christian commitment embodies a way of interrelating values and experience, of applying social utilities realizable only in the long-term future to the alternatives of present choice, and of coping with the material threats of open-ended uncertainty. The Christian commitment provides the ongoing structure for human interrelationships, the framework guiding the search for ultimate meaning and overriding obligation without which these interrelationships degenerate into mutual exploitation and social havoc. Variations in understandings of ultimate meaning and obligation are to be expected, and to an extent these are being searched out by survey methods. A guess as to findings is that when sufficient evidence is at hand the variations will be found as great within communcant groups as between them.

It is suggested here that the essential framework of values guiding the society's quest for ultimate meaning and obligation is an attribute of the general community. Centered in this framework is the ethical inheritance of the Judaic-Christian tradition. Roman Catholic and Episcopal components of the common Christian community would not be expected to have differences involving these elements of the basic Christian belief system. If the ongoing consultations between the two communions can be taken as reliable indicators of the state of theological understanding, basic complementarity, if not substantial agreement, can be inferred. Such differences as are sensed would seem to be rooted in the modes of verbal expression and in historic accumulations of misunderstandings of the meaning of language, rather than in the central truths these expressions were originally intended to convey. If these observations can be accepted as working assumptions, it is possible to start with the premise that the central elements of Christian belief and of ethcal obligation are sufficently shared by the two communions that any paired parishes are living within the same belief system. Any differences between them are then likely to result from the operation of two familiar mechanisms, displacement and substitution.

Displacement occurs when, in the behavior of the group concerned, a set of higher and often abstract values is displaced by specific, tangible and expressive imperatives that may or may not be durable and reliable embodiments of the higher values. These imperatives in time acquire their own value content, which assumes primary salience, while the higher values from which they are assumed to stem lose both meaning and visibility. For most people, the ideas of ultimate meaning and overriding obligation are highly subjective. Forms and styles of objective embodiment are essential to their comprehension. Thus there is an understandable tendency to rely upon shared modes for concretizing these abstractions. The acting out of expressive symbolism in ritualized forms is a way of renewing commitment to, and confidence in the subjective values thus symbolized. But this process, essential though it is, can also substitute an attachment to the expressive styles for a conscious renewal of commitment to the higher values. It need scarcely be added that expressive styles can also, over time, undergo types of elaboration and adaptation (both in the technical sense) that strain their connections with the higher value system.

These observations about ritualized styles of behavior are by no means limited in their application to worship and church discipline. Displacement is widely observable in the contemporary society in accepted conventions of social behavior, as evidencing adherence on the part of the actor to some set of attributed higher values.

Another way of describing the impact of displacement is to say that within a general system of belief there can be subsystems for the expression of beliefs. These subsystems may differ from each other in content, style and emphasis. There are familiar examples of subsystem differences around the world within the same communion. Such differences can also be found among parishes of the same communion in the United States. The consequences of subsystem differences can be thought of as falling along a range. At one extreme they are complementary and mutually supporting. At the other they produce so much social conflict that virtual incompatibility results. The location of paired parishes along this range would indicate the extent to which styles of displacement raise obstacles to capacity to function as a coherent Christian community, with a shared perception of a common Christian identity.

Substitution, the second familiar mechanism, affects voluntary organizations in particular, and is characterized by a type of often subtle introversion. It refers to the tendency of an organization to replace those higher values it presumably exists to express with an attachment to the satisfactions experienced by its members in sharing an elite social status, community prestige, a special cultural tradition, and the like. Thus a local parish may be perceived as a power center, a community social or service club, a culture-preserving group, or some combination of these. Substitution is most likely to develop in organizations with non-operational goals, which in this sense means when the outcomes of the organization's purpose can be perceived only remotely, if at all, by the members. The member then tends to identify himself with other, more readily identifiable characteristics of the organization to which he can attribute positive satisfactions. Where these tendencies control the membership, the real values of the organization shift away from the higher values, and cluster around the preservation of the set of special internalized characteristics. Whenever a tendency toward substitution controls the sense of parish identity and purpose, the parish capacity for relating itself effectively to the larger Christian community is seriously impaired. The basic parish values in effect center around considerations irrelevant to the parish's reason for being.

To summarize, in the religious organization, the belief system is central. It comes to grips with the ultimate meaning, the questions of life and death, of injury and illness, of interpersonal relations, and all the other issues that distinguish life in a jungle of mutual exploitation from the life of Christian love. The belief system needs expression in forms of action, of which some, often symbolic, refresh the sense of commitment to the goal, and others, direct and specific, aim to produce in the world the values embodied in the system. But religious organizations are peculiarly subject to both displacement and substitution. Both tendencies particularize the organization, and make it and its participants less capable of unified participation in a larger community of conviction and commitment. In any context where the possibility of a unified parish is to be considered, the state of the belief system will need careful analysis and evaluation.

2. Expressive Action

Expressive action in this connection means "doing the things you believe in." In the American culture in particular, some form of "doing" is essential to the confidence that subjective values have present meaning and reality. Also, and vitally important, the felt experience of having expressed a set of values in some structured action generates satisfactions which stimulate a tendency to feed more energy into organizational participation, thereby augmenting satisfactions. The higher the satisfaction, the more likely it is to be pursued aggressively; the lower the satisfaction, the more likely its displacement by other kinds of gratifications. The working assumption is that a unified Christian community must be able to engage in shared, cooperative action, action expressive of its beliefs and commitment. This is essential to organic vitality. In each situation of paired parishes, the question will be whether the capability for such action is present.

Expressive action is of two major types. One type is internalized in the sense that it is contained within the membership and serves the purpose of generating, through this interaction, the energy needed for the continuing life of the organization and for the expression of its values in the general society. The other type is external expression, action influencing the general society. Both types appear to be essential to organization health.

The function of internalized expressive action is the refreshing of the sense of common identification and goal-seeking, the perception of community, the linkages with long tradition, and the commitment to external expressive action. This is the point at which structured internal interaction generates the energies that are projected to external expression. While it would seem that a variety of styles of internal expression can be employed concurrently, this variety cannot go so far as to splinter or fragment the community with a diversity of mutually inconsistent identifications. It is suggested that the equilibrium of variety and unity may be maintained by open and visible mobility of the members of the community. For example, services of worship should be open to full participation by all members. There should be no overt or subtle elitism which admits some members to some forms of participation, but excludes others. It is important also that the roles of the clergy be mobile, so that all are equally qualified and eligible to exercise all of the roles of the ordained person.

This is the point at which serious difficulties can arise. If traditional policies remain so closed that the dynamic interaction of the full community is impossible, weaknesses seem unavoidable. To put the point more explicitly, segregated Sacraments, such as the Holy Eucharist, open to some members of the community but closed to others, are fragmenting influences. Clergy qualified to exercise their roles in some, but not all, of the community action cannot be fully effective in symbolizing to the community the essential unity of belief and commitment. The full potential of internal expressive action, so it would seem, cannot be realized short of intercommunion and the mutual acceptance of the efficacy of Holy Orders. Without these steps the community cannot act as a coherent social organism in the renewal of its conviction and commitment. As long as this unity is not possible in any formally recognized way, compromises will be necessary, attempting to symbolize unity without actually expressing it. Of course, it is entirely possible that the sense of community will develop in any case, with the result that members will override the formal barriers and participate as they are moved to do. If that occurs, the formal order becomes artificial, and any effort to restore it will be divisive.

Altogether, it would seem that the problem of community-wide internal expression, and especially sacramental expression, may be the critical aspect of design. This concern needs much more analysis than is sketched here. It is the point at which a significant break-through is needed.

The second type of expressive action is external in nature, action which transmits and applies the Christian commitment to the general community, and indeed to the world, of which the special Christian community is a part. Such action seems initially to take two forms. One is found in the participation of the individual in the interaction patterns of the larger community. The other is through Christian community undertakings aimed at the problems and needs of the external society.

A strong case can be made that the primary impact of the Christian commitment upon the general society is through the first form, the participation of the individual in societal interactions of a generalized, non-ecclesiastical character. The high energy interactions of the society are those producing the decision-influencing and decision-making in what can be broadly characterized as the secular world. These are social interactions in that individuals and groups, by problem-solving or bargaining strategies, attempt to resolve their perceived dilemmas of choice. Participants in these processes feed their values into their interaction patterns. Indeed, their values energize their efforts to produce one or another outcome. It follows that committed Christians do perceive the questions they face as involving the application of the Christian ethic, and, with others sensing the same relevance, rely upon this commitment to set the framework for their decisions. The major responsibility of the church is to develop in the individual, who lives in a complex of multiple societal roles, a reliable sense of the application of the Christian commitment to the way he lives his roles. How this is done, in terms of attitude and sensitivity building, will not be examined here. It is enough to identify this most important channel for expressive action.

The second form of external action involves activities undertaken by the church itself. Here it is important to put aside the activities that are internal institution-building, and look only at those that express impacts externally upon the general society. It must be recognized that church efforts of this kind, in this society, tend to be low-energy compared with those underpinned by the resources of the general society. The church cannot expect to match the energy available to the economic sector and to the polity. It must apply its scarce resources with a strategy of influence, of guiding the attention of the higher energy systems to the problems that demand solution, and to the ways by which these problems can be solved. In this sense the role of the church may be seen as innovating and experimental, a matter of developing the framework within which societal problem resolution can proceed with confidence. It can be argued, in this connection, that the church has pioneered the development of societal action in education, in the care of the ill, and in the amelioration of poverty.

The positive expression of commitment by the Christian community can be seen, then, as having these two aspects. On the one hand, the people of the church, as actors in general societal interaction, project their values into societal decision-making. The church develops its people to play their parts confidently and reliably. On the other hand, the church undertakes a limited number of pioneering, experimental, standard-setting efforts to point the way that general society efforts can take. Any vital Christian community must have the predispositions and the capacities to undertake these forms of expressive action. Unless these elements exist, the requisites of community are not present.

3. Physical Space

A unified Christian community requires a location in physical and social space. This means a base of operations, a place where common worship, social interactions, and cooperative expression are carried on. Multiple locations are often feasible, but it seems essential to have at least a symbolic center of attention. Such a symbol reenforces the sense of shared identity. This point will not be further developed here. Clearly, different polities are committed to rather different ways of acquiring, developing, and holding physical properties. Problems may arise in this connection. A highly practical consideration is that all groups within the special community must be disposed to open the use of their properties to full and equal use by the community as a whole. One of the needs to be tested is whether this disposition exists.

4. Commitment of Support

Without the input of economic support, the unified Christian community cannot maintain its physical existence. This point is self-evident. Properties cannot be maintained, clerical and lay staff cannot be retained, operating cost cannot be met without monetary contributions by the people of the community. Will the people support a unified Christian community? Do they put a sufficiently high value upon the expected consequences of being one in essence to commit themselves to underwriting costs? Attitudes toward economic support need to be tested. Any of several outcomes seems possible. A projected pattern of action, involving wide participation by the people of the community in innovative services to the wider community might stimulate a willingness to increase contributions. It might also alienate contributions. Some persons might regard a unified parish as a betrayal of cherished tradition. Others might see it as an exciting step toward new relevance. The patterns of interest and disposition need to be tested and evaluated.

Summary: This is a tentative and preliminary effort to identify the salient attributes and variables characterizing the Christian community. The assumption is that any approach to design in the specific case must start with an analysis of the state of these attributes, and of the variables that presumably make the difference between an effective undertaking and a failure.

An Approach to Testing and Measurement

A framework of ideas about the nature of the Christian community has been projected. If that pattern of assumptions can be accepted as a working base, an approach can be designed for testing whether the assumed attributes of community are present in a particular situation. The procedure, while far from easy, is reasonably clear-cut. The pattern of attributes, each with its critical subsidiary variables, would be used as the base for diagnostic probes, testing the presence of the attributes of community and the influence of the variables. This is the type of analysis to which the survey research strategy is uniquely adapted. The special design would be difficult and time-consuming. Testing and validation of the instrument would be necessary. The result would be a way of building profiles of Roman Catholic and Episcopal parishes, and for comparing these profiles in terms of possibilities for interrelating pairs of parishes in unified Christian communities.

The analysis of these profiles could disclose the extent to which the basic ingredients of community are shared by the two parish groups. The nature, and the strength, of diverging influences could be identified by the state of the variable factors in each group. The outcome of such analysis might be a decision to press toward unification, or to leave the situation undisturbed. It is possible that an induced growth process might be indicated, to develop common perceptions and expectations, and to reduce the influence of dysfunctional variables. The stimulation of shared action in external expressive activities might be seen as a constructive step in an incremental strategy toward the unified community. Considerations of timing, priority and relative emphasis in alternative approaches could be weighed. The specific steps in analysis would become evident as the result of a battery of experimental applications of the diagnostic profile. In this way also it should be possible to verify what barriers to the unified community actually exist, whether these barriers are the ones presumed to exist, and how deeply rooted these obstacles might be in a particular situation.

Altogether, what is suggested here for exploratory discussion is an objective approach to the analysis of present realities in a number of sample situations, to determine the potentialities of steps toward developing unified Christian communities. The critical obstacles to unity in parish life could be identified, and the path for a strategy of unification could be projected. These considerations are now at the level of conjecture. Attention lingers with differences in tradition and polity, rather than upon the degree of shared commitment and predisposition toward expressive action. The potential of the grass-roots dynamics needs systematic exploration.

Can Barriers to Unity be Modified by Inducing Change?

The complexities posed by this question are beyond any adequate treatment here. The very tentative suggestions that follow are hazarded as lines for further exploration.

But it can be said with some confidence that any highly structured, stereotyped treatment of interparish attributes would probably be ineffective, and might be disastrous. Rather, evaluation of the potential for unity would be comparative analysis and interpretation of the profiles of the two parishes. This would identify the elements in each parish that pose barriers to realizing the objective. No doubt some situations would show very little potential and would be put aside. Others would be highly promising. The greater number would fall somewhere between the two extremes.

The specific findings in each situation would indicate the direction, and also the complexity, of the effort at inducing change. For example, and these suggestions are largely speculative, the barriers may be primarily those of "sunk costs" in physical structures and facilities, while also present are strong identities in belief and disposition to expressive action. Such a situation is quite favorable, because a problem-solving strategy can be employed. In other situations the barriers may be essentially cognitive, in the way attributes of the parishes and of their communions are perceived. For these, a strategy of reconstructing perceptions may be indicated, without pushing movement toward unification at the same time. Shared perceptions and shared meanings, ranging from forms of ritual through physical symbols to the effect of Christian commitment upon personal decisions may build the indispensable foundation of a new social structure. In still other instances, disparate value patterns may be evident. These would be the most difficult situations. Much would depend upon how deeply-rooted the values are, and what they represent by way of different ideas about Christianity and the church. Efforts at inducing change in such situations would be long term and high-risk.

What are the means of stimulating change? An analogy can be suggested. Considerable research effort is being directed at present toward the general problem of organizational development. It is pointed to the question of how an organization can be stimulated and reenforced in the effort to realize its capabilities more completely and more effectively. This is to say that analogies may be available. This paper will not go beyond that suggestion.

Summary

This has been an experimental effort to explore the path toward realizing unified Roman Catholic-Episcopal parishes. Some essential attributes of a unified parish are examined: the Christian belief system, the disposition to expressive action, disposition to joint utilization of social and physical space, and readiness to provide essential economic support. It is suggested that a detailed analytical design can be developed and validated to test and measure the current state of each of these attributes in paired parishes. The result could be a set of parish profiles, showing the relationships of the parishes with respect to the critical variables. Finally, it is suggested that approaches may be increasingly available from the field of organizational development to guide and reenforce efforts toward surmounting the identified barriers to unity. The implicit starting point, of course, is an environment in which such movements toward unity are possible. This means a continued, even accelerated effort at building the necessary foundations. These necessary foundations would seem to be intercommunion, the mutual recognition and acceptance of Orders, the compatibility of discipline, and parish freedom to search and experiment with interrelationship.

BIOGRAPHIES

HERBERT J. RYAN, S.J.

Herbert J. Ryan, S.J., was born in Scarsdale, New York, in 1931. He entered the Society of Jesus in 1949 and was ordained to the priesthood in 1962. Father Ryan earned his doctorate in theology from Rome's Gregorian University and is presently Professor of Historical Theology at Woodstock College, New York City. Father Ryan is a member of both the international (ARCIC) and national (ARC) official Anglican-Roman Catholic dialogues.

STEPHEN F. BAYNE, JR.

The Rt. Rev. Stephen F. Bayne, Jr., was born in Manhattan in 1908. Following ordination, he remained as a Fellow and Tutor of the General Theological Seminary (N.Y.C.) for two years, then served as a parish priest in St. Louis and in Northampton, Mass. In 1941 he was appointed Chaplain of Columbia University where he remained, interrupted by two years as a Navy chaplain, until 1947 when he was consecrated Bishop of Olympia (western Washington). On January 1, 1960, he became the Anglican Communion's first world-wide Executive Officer. At the end of 1964 he was appointed First Vice-President of the Episcopal Church's Executive Council. In mid-1970 he returned to the General Seminary as professor and now Dean. The author of many books, Bishop Bayne is widely known as "Mr. Anglican."

ARTHUR A. VOGEL

The Rt. Rev. Arthur A. Vogel, Bishop Coadjutor of West Missouri, is a member of both the international (ARCIC) and national (ARC) official Anglican-Roman Catholic dialogues as well as of the Joint Commission on Ecumenical Relations of the Episcopal Church. He is also a delegate to the Consultation on Church Union (COCU). Born in 1924, he took his Ph.D. from Harvard in 1952. He taught theology at Nashotah House (Wisconsin) from 1952-1971, where he was sub-dean. The author of five books and numerous articles, Bishop Vogel has been a delegate to every General Convention of the Episcopal Church since 1955.

BIOGRAPHIES

AVERY DULLES, S.J.

Rev. Avery Dulles, S.J., born 1918, graduated from Harvard College in 1940. After service as a Naval Officer in World War II, he entered the Jesuits in 1946, was ordained to the priesthood in 1956, and earned his doctorate in theology from the Gregorian University in Rome in 1960. Since that time he has taught Systematic Theology at Woodstock College, first in Maryland and, since 1970, in New York City. He is the author of eight books and numerous articles on theology. His most recent books are *The Survival of Dogma* (Doubleday) and *A History of Apologetics* (Westminster), both published in 1971. Father Dulles presently serves on the Board of Trustees of Fordham University and on the Board of Directors of the Catholic Theological Society of America, and he has taken part in many bilateral consultations in the United States, including the Lutheran/Roman Catholic and the Anglican/Roman Catholic conversations.

THOMAS J. TALLEY

Born 1924 in Texas and ordained priest in 1952, the Rev. Thomas J. Talley took his Th.D. from the General Theological Seminary (N.Y.C.) where he is now Professor of Liturgics. He served parishes in Texas from 1951-1961, and taught at Nashotah House (Wisconsin) from 1963-1971. In the Episcopal Diocese of Dallas he was chairman of the diocesan department of ecumenical relations, and he has been recently engaged in the ecumenical aspects of liturgical renewal.

JOHN GALLEN, S.J.

John Gallen, S.J., was born in New York City in 1933. He entered the Society of Jesus in 1950 and was ordained in 1963. In 1967 he received his doctorate in theology from the University of Trier (Germany) and is presently Professor of Pastoral Theology at Woodstock College, New York City.

REGINALD H. FULLER

Born in Horsham (Sussex, England) in 1915 and educated at Cambridge University, the Rev. Reginald H. Fuller served as curate in three English parishes for six years. He taught on the faculties of the Queen's College (Birmingham, England), St. David's College (Lampeter, Wales) and Seabury-Western Seminary (Evanston, Illinois) before becoming Baldwin Professor of Sacred Literature at the Union Theological Seminary (N.Y.C.) in 1966. He is author of twelve books on the New Testament and related fields, a translator of Bonhoeffer, Bultmann, and Jeremias from the German, a member of the Episcopal Church's Committee on Prayer Book Revision (Lectionary and Calendar), and Episcopalian representative to the official dialogues with Lutherans both in the U.S.A. and on the international level. In 1972 he became Professor of New Testament at the Virginia Theological Seminary in Alexandria, Va. His latest book (forthcoming) is *The Formation of the Resurrection Narratives.*

JOHN LINNAN, C.S.V.

Rev. John E. Linnan, C.S.V., received his doctorate in theology from the University of Louvain (Belgium) in 1965, writing his dissertation on John Henry Newman. He is currently Associate Professor of Theology at the Washington Theological Coalition in Washington, D.C.

HENRY G. J. BECK

Msgr. Henry G. J. Beck studied theology in Italy and France and received his doctorate in 1948 from the Gregorian University in Rome. Since 1940 he has taught church history at Immaculate Conception Seminary, Darlington, N.J. Pius XII appointed him papal chamberlain in 1958 and in 1965 Paul VI named him domestic prelate. The author of many works, he was editor in medieval history for the *New Catholic Encyclopedia.* At Vatican Council II he served as theologian to the Bishops of Bridgeport and Charleston. He is a member of the official Roman Catholic dialogue with the Presbyterian and Reformed Churches. Msgr. Beck is currently pastor of Sacred Heart Church, Lyndhurst, N.J.

J. ROBERT WRIGHT

Born 1936 and ordained priest in 1964, the Rev. J. Robert Wright took his D.Phil. from Oxford University in 1967. He taught at the Episcopal Theological School (Cambridge, Mass.) 1966-1968. He then joined the faculty of the General Theological Seminary (N.Y.C.), where he is now Professor of Ecclesiastical History. He is a member of the national Anglican-Roman Catholic Consultation (ARC) and also participates in the Episcopal Church's dialogue with the Eastern Orthodox.

WILLIAM F. MURPHY

Rev. William F. Murphy is Instructor in Theological Studies at Emmanuel College, Boston. Currently he is a candidate for Doctor of Theology at the Gregorian University in Rome, specializing in ecumenics and ecclesiology. In addition to work in Roman Catholic parishes in Boston, he has been a member of the Archdiocesan Ecumenical Commission there.

RICHARD GARY

The Rev. Richard Gary has been Planning Officer for the Episcopal Diocese of New York since 1970. Born in 1924, he did his theological studies at Yale Divinity School. For eleven years he served as priest-in-charge of St. Mary's, Manhattanville (West Harlem, N.Y.C.).

EUGENE J. SCHALLERT, S.J.

Rev. Eugene J. Schallert, S.J., is Director of the Institute for Socio-Religious Research at the University of San Francisco. After completion of graduate studies in Sociology at Fordham University in N.Y.C., Father Schallert joined the Department of Sociology at the University of San Francisco. Since 1960 he has been doing research in a wide variety of sociological areas but his primary interest has been in the Sociology of Religion. He has published four books as well as a large number of monographs and articles.

GEORGE A. SHIPMAN

Dr. George A. Shipman is Professor of Public Affairs and Political Science in the Graduate School of Public Affairs at the University of Washington, Seattle. His doctorate is from Cornell University. Before joining the Washington faculty he served at West Virginia University, in research at Princeton, and at Duke. He has engaged in governmental research and consultation, and was in the Federal civilian service during World War II. His primary professional field is organization design and analysis. As an Episcopal layman, he has been a vestryman and senior warden in his parish, delegate to diocesan convention, member of diocesan council, and deputy to General Convention. He is a member of the Standing Committee on Program and Budget, the Episcopalian delegations to the Consultation on Church Union (COCU) and to the Anglican-Roman Catholic Consultation in the U.S.A. (ARC), and the General Board of Examining Chaplains.

REFERENCES

NEW DYNAMICS OF ANGLICAN-ROMAN CATHOLIC
DIALOGUE — Herbert J. Ryan, S.J.

1. *Documents on Anglican/Roman Catholic Relations*. United States Catholic Conference, Washington, D.C., 1972, 9-20. Hereafter this book will be referred to as A/RC Doc.
2. A/RC Doc., 23.
3. *Ibid.*, 23-25.
4. *Ibid.*, 13.
5. *Ibid.*, 13.
6. The text of this statement may be found in *Ecumenical Trends* I-2 (May, 1972), 5-8; *Theology* LXXV-622 (April, 1972), 187-190; *Catholic Mind* LXX-1262 (April, 1972), 61-64.
7. This form of ecclesiology is specifically mentioned by Cardinal Willebrands in his important address at Great St. Mary's, Cambridge, England, on January 18, 1970. The full text is in A/RC Doc., 32-41. A more detailed analysis of this theology of the Church may be found in Jerome Hamer, O.P., *The Church is a Communion*. Geoffrey Chapman, London, 1964; and Emmanuel Lanne, O.S.B., "Pluralism and Unity—The Possibility of a Variety of Typologies within the same Ecclesial Allegiance," *One in Christ*, vi-3 (1970), 430-451.

REFERENCES

8. This took place at Immacolata Retreat House, Liberty, Missouri, from Monday, May 25, until Thursday, May 28, 1970. Two Archbishops and twenty-one Bishops attended.
9. Perhaps the widest attendance was achieved in New York through the use of closed circuit TV on May 17, 1971. It is estimated that over 600 diocesan clergy took part in the conference which was held simultaneously in 21 centers.
10. The conference held at Narraganset, Rhode Island, October 8-9, 1971 had representatives from all the Episcopal and Roman Catholic dioceses of the area.
11. Three excellent examples of diocesan dialogue groups are those in Bridgeport, Providence and New York.
12. Cf. footnote 1.
13. This concept originated with two parishes in Southbridge, Mass. Hopefully, it will spread throughout the dioceses of Worcester and Western Mass. A conference for the Bishops and clergy of both dioceses was held on Feb. 1, 1972 at Notre Dame, Southbridge, and the concept received enthusiastic support of the Bishops and the many clergy attending.
14. *Catholic Mind* LXIX-1252 (April, 1971), 35-50.
15. Herbert J. Ryan, S.J., "Anglican-Roman Catholic Doctrinal Agreement on the Eucharist," *Worship* XLVI-1 (January, 1972), 7-8.
16. Cf. Herbert J. Ryan, S.J., "Lambeth '68: A Roman Catholic Theological Reflection," *Theological Studies* XXIX-4 (December, 1968), 597-636.
17. "Report of the Anglican-Roman Catholic Joint Preparatory Commission" in *Lambeth Conference 1968: Documents on Anglican-Roman Catholic Relations.* The Talbot Press, Saffron Walden, Essex, 1968, #19 (Malta Report).

REFLECTIONS ON DOCTRINAL AGREEMENT

Avery Dulles, S.J.

1. Text in *Documents on Anglican/Roman Catholic Relations* (Washington, D.C.: USCC, 1972), p. 18.
2. "Integralism" or "integrism" receives its name from an anti-

Modernist reactionary movement that flourished in Roman Catholicism between 1907 and 1921. Subsequently the term has come to designate a mentality that goes far beyond the historical framework of the Modernist crisis. This mentality tends to overextend the realm of certitude by exaggerated appeals to authority and thus to condemn openness, research, and the questioning of received opinions. An excellent discussion of "Integrism" may be found in Y. Congar, *Vrai et fausse Réforme dans l'Eglise* (Paris: Cerf, 1950), Appendix 3, pp. 604-22.

3. This position is far older and more complex than the Fundamentalism of early twentieth century Protestantism. Gustave Thils calls Pierre Jurieu the leading theoretician of the "fundamental articles." "By fundamental points," wrote Jurieu, "we understand certain general principles of the Christian religion which must be believed by distinct faith in order for one to be saved and to be called Christian," *Traité de l'unité de l'Eglise et des points fondamentaux contre M. Nicole* (Rotterdam, 1688), cited by G. Thils, *Histoire doctrinale du mouvement oecuménique* (Louvain: Warny, new ed., 1962), p. 192.

4. "The issue between Alexandrians and Antiochians was not simply a question of words but of two conceptions of the mystery of the Incarnation that could be called almost opposed even if, in addition, they are complementary," writes E. Lanne, "Les différences compatibles avec l'unité dans la tradition de l'Eglise ancienne (Jusqu'au XIIe siècle)," *Istina* 8 (1961-62), pp. 227-56, p. 247.

5. "5. If anyone do not truly and rightly confess with the Fathers *one incarnate nature of the divine Word,* whereby the term 'incarnate' means that our substance is perfect and undiminished in Christ God but without sin — *condemnatus sit.*"

"6. If anyone do not truly and rightly confess with the Fathers that one and the same *Lord and God, Jesus Christ is of and in two natures substantially united* but distinct and undivided — *condemnatus sit.*"

Joseph Neuner and H. Roos (eds.), *The Teaching of the Catholic Church* (Staten Island: Alba House, 1967), nos. 271-72. For Latin text see Denzinger-Schönmetzer, *Enchi-*

REFERENCES

ridion symbolorum (32nd. ed., Freiburg: Herder, 1963), nos. 505-6. I am following here the interpretation of E. Lanne, art. cit., p. 250.

6. Cf. K. Rahner, "Der Pluralismus in der Theologie und die Einheit des Bekenntnisses in der Kirche," *Schriften zur Theologie,* vol. 9 (Einsiedeln: Benziger, 1970), pp. 11-33. Bernard Lonergan in his *Doctrinal Pluralism* (Milwaukee: Marquette Univ., 1971) takes a similar position.
7. These words are quoted from the admirable statement on comprehensiveness in the Report of Section III ("The Renewal of the Church in Unity") of *The Lambeth Conference 1968, Resolutions and Reports* (New York: Seabury Press, 1968), pp. 140-41.
8. Rahner, *art. cit.,* pp. 32-33.
9. A keen awareness of this problem is evident in R. E. Brown, "The Virginal Conception of Jesus," *Theological Studies* 33/1 (March 1972), pp. 1-34.
10. Seeking to clarify the logical implications of anathemas Anselm Atkins correctly notes: "It is not logically necessary that *all* the propositions into which the condemned statement is analyzable are false. The most an anathema *need* say is that a certain verbal statement is analyzable into at least *one* false proposition," "Religious Assertions and Doctrinal Development," *Theological Studies* 27 (1966), pp. 523-52, p. 532.
11. Denzinger-Schönmetzer, *op. cit.,* no. 407.
12. *Ibid.,* no. 902.
13. Gregory Baum, after adverting to the complete silence of Vatican II on the matter of indulgences, observes that this practice in many cases has "ceased to play any role whatever in the spiritual life of the Christian" and concludes that if one "believes that the gaining of indulgences does not help Christians of our day to enter more intelligently, actively and easily into the process of complete reconciliation with their Lord, then he may legitimately hope that the granting of indulgences will be discontinued in the Church." "Silence on Indulgences," *The Ecumenist* 3/3 (March-April 1965), pp. 37-39.
14. Edmund Schlink, *The Coming Christ and the Coming Church* (Edinburg: Oliver & Boyd, 1967), p. 80.

15. Cf. Vatican II, *Unitatis redintegratio*, no. 14; in W. M. Abbott (ed.), *Documents of Vatican II* (New York: America Press, 1966), p. 358.
16. Vatican II, *Ad gentes*, no. 22; Abbott, op. cit., p. 612.
17. Vatican II, *Gaudium et spes*, no. 44; Abbott, op. cit., p. 246.
18. Vatican II, *Unitatis redintegratio*, no. 17; Abbott, op. cit., p. 360.
19. *The Lambeth Conference of 1968*, p. 29.
20. M. Wiles, *The Making of Christian Doctrine* (Cambridge: University Press, 1967), p. 177.
21. See for example the remarks of Hans Küng in *The Council, Reform and Reunion* (New York: Sheed & Ward, 1962), p. 6. Vatican II explicitly recognized that church renewal "has notable ecumenical importance," *Unitatis Redintegratio*, no. 6; Abbott, *op. cit.*, p. 351.
22. Cf. Herbert J. Ryan, "Lambeth '68: A Roman Catholic Reflection," *Theological Studies* 29/4 (Dec. 1968), p. 597-98.
23. The Windsor Statement on the Eucharist (Sept. 1971) consciously seeks to achieve the first two of these three goals: "We believe that we have reached substantial agreement on the doctrine of the eucharist. . . . It is our hope that in view of the agreement we have reached on eucharistic faith, this doctrine will no longer constitute an obstacle to the unity we seek," no. 12, text in *Documents on Anglican/Roman Catholic Relations*, p. 50. Further assessment by the churches will be needed to determine whether the lack of explicit mention of the sacrificial character of the eucharist, the omission in the text of the term "transubstantiation," and the particular expressions adopted for affirming the real presence — to mention but three controversial points — are in fact considered satisfactory to Roman Catholic and Anglican Christians today.
24. Cf. A. Dulles, *The Survival of Dogma* (New York: Doubleday, 1971), pp. 162-63, 167.
25. Cardinal Willebrands' Address in Cambridge, England, Jan. 18, 1970; text in *Documents on Anglican/Roman Catholic Relations*, p. 36. It is very significant that Cardinal Willebrands in this address, like E. Lanne, to whose work he refers, includes in the notion of an ecclesial *typos* "a characteristic theological method and approach" (p. 39).

REFERENCES

LITURGICAL CONVERGENCE (ANGLICAN VIEW)

Thomas J. Talley

1. *Constitution on the Sacred Liturgy*, 10.
2. A commission was given to the bishops of Scotland to frame a liturgy for that country by Charles I on May 13, 1634.
3. *Constitution on the Sacred Liturgy*, 22.2.
4. Adopted by ARC XI, January 23, 1972. Text in *Ecumenical Trends* I-2 (May, 1972), 7.
5. Const. Apost. "*Sacramentum ordinis*," Nov. 30, 1947. (Denz. 2301.)

LITURGICAL CONVERGENCE (CATHOLIC VIEW)

John Gallen, S.J.

1. Jean-Marie Tillard, "The Bread and the Cup of Reconciliation," *Sacramental Reconciliation* (*Concilium* 61), ed. Edward Schillebeeckx. New York: Herder and Herder, 1971, p. 47. See also his "Pénitence et Eucharistie," *LaMaison-Dieu* 90, (1967) 103-131.
2. Elmer Arndt, *The Font and the Table*. Richmond: John Knox Press, 1967, p. 71.
3. Tillard, *La Maison-Dieu* 90, *art. cit.*, p. 105.

THE MINISTRY IN THE NEW TESTAMENT

Reginald H. Fuller

1. Following suggestions of D. Georgei, *Die Gegner der Paulus im 2. Korintherbrief* (Neukirchen, 1964) and G. Friedrich, "Die Gegner der Paulus im 2. Korintherbrief" in *Abraham unser Vater: Festschrift für O. Michel,* ed. O. Betz, M. Hengel and P. Schmidt (Leiden/Köln, 1963).
2. Since this community was much involved in collecting funds for Paul, the hardening of these administrative functions into quasi-permanent offices is intelligible.
3. A. Richardson, ed., *A Theological Wordbook of the Bible* (London, 1950), s.v. "Minister, Ministry."

4. B. S. Easton, *The Pastoral Epistles* (London, 1948). (Guttunger, 1951).
5. B. Lohse, *Die Ordination im Spätjudentum (und in Neuen Testament)*.
6. That is, the *office* of *presbuteroi*, a combined office of teaching and government. The name *presbuteroi* originated elsewhere, in the Palestinian churches, where it designated functionaries who governed but apparently did not minister the word.
7. For the relevance of this logion to church order see my *The Mission and Achievement of Jesus* (London, 1967), p. 57. If this reformulation of the Jesus saying is tradition, rather than Lucan redaction, it could well represent a phase similar to that in Hebrews. In that case the more developed church order implied in Acts 14 and 20 (see below) will belong to the level of Lucan redaction.
8. What we would now-a-days call the laity. That word used in its modern sense is inapplicable to the New Testament. All Christians are members of the *laos* and therefore "laity," including ministers.
9. F. Buchsel, *Th WB* II 909 (my translation: cf. *TDNT* II).
10. This coining of a christological title from a ministerial office raises the question whether 1 Peter 2:25, from the baptismal homily, indicates that already at the earlier stage the titles "shepherd" and *episcopos* were coming into use for the still free charismatic ministers of the word.
11. Cf. already B. S. Easton, op. cit., p. 226: "It is therefore an anachronism when Acts tells us that Paul and Barnabas 'appointed elders in every Church' (14:23) or gives the technical title to the leaders of the congregation in Ephesus (20:17)." The work on Acts done since 1948 by Ernst Haenchen and John Knox confirms the rightness of Easton's position.
12. For the meaning of *cheirotonein* see C. H. Turner in *The Early History of the Church and Ministry*, ed. H. B. Swete (London, 1921), pp. 208-210.
13. See John Knox, *Chapters in a Life of Paul* (London, 1954); G. Bornkamm, *Paul* (New York, 1971), pp. xiii-xxviii. I note a reluctance among Catholic biblical scholars to accept the full implications of this methodological principle.

REFERENCES

14. So, e.g., G. Bornkamm, *ThWB* VI 667f. English translation in *TDNT* VI, 667.
15. For the *Bishofsspiegel* see H. W. Bartsch, *Die Anfänge urchristlichen Rechtsbildungen* (Hamburg, 1965), pp. 82ff.
16. E. Schlink, *The Coming Christ and the Coming Church* (Edinburgh/London, 1967), p. 207.
17. Such was the conclusion of B. H. Streeter, *The Primitive Church* (London, 1930), p. ix.
18. *The Lambeth Conference 1930* (London, 1930), p. 115.

ROMAN CATHOLIC VIEWS ON ORDAINED MINISTRY

John Linnan, C.S.V.

1. Francis Clark, S.J., *Anglican Orders and Defect of Intention* (London, 1956); and *Eucharistic Sacrifice and the Reformation* (Westminister, Md., 1960).
2. John Jay Hughes, *Absolutely Null and Utterly Void* (Washington, 1968); and *Stewards of the Lord* (London, 1970).
3. Edward P. Echlin, S.J., *The Anglican Eucharist in Ecumenical Perspective* (New York, 1970).
4. John Jay Hughes, *Absolutely Null and Utterly Void*, p. 284.
5. Vatican II, *Lumen Gentium*, no. 15; in Walter M. Abbott, S.J. (ed.), *Documents of Vatican II* (New York, 1966), pp. 33-34; and Vatican II, *Unitatis Redintegratio*, no. 19; Abbott, *op. cit.*, pp. 361-362.
6. Daniel O'Hanlon, S.J., "A New Approach to the Validity of Church Orders," in *Reconsiderations: Roman Catholic/Presbyterian and Reformed Theological Conversations, 1966-1967* (New York, 1967), pp. 140-144.
7. Vatican II, *Lumen Gentium*, no. 8; Abbott, *op. cit.*, p. 23.
8. Franz Jozef Van Beeck, S.J., "Towards an Ecumenical Understanding of the Sacraments," *Journal of Ecumenical Studies*, vol. 3 (1966), pp. 57-112.
9. Van Beeck, *op. cit.*, p. 63.
10. *Ibid*, pp. 85-86, n. 52.
11. O'Hanlon, *op. cit.*, p. 145. O'Hanlon's article is based on the position of Van Beeck.

233

12. Van Beeck, *op. cit.*, pp. 88-89.
13. *Ibid*, p. 90.
14. *Ibid*, p. 105.
15. *Ibid*, pp. 104-105.
16. Kilian McDonnell, "Ways of Validating Ministry," *Journal of Ecumenical Studies,* vol. 7 (1970), pp. 209-265.
17. *Ibid*, p. 217.
18. *Ibid*, p. 244.
19. *Ibid*, p. 250.
20. *Ibid*.
21. *Ibid*, pp. 253-254.
22. *Ibid*, p. 254.
23. Vatican II, *Lumen Gentium*, no. 8; Abbott, *op. cit.*, p. 23.
24. Vatican II, *Unitatis Redintegratio*, no. 19; Abbott, *op. cit.*, p. 361.
25. McDonnell, *op. cit.*, p. 257.
26. *Ibid*, p. 258.
27. Van Beeck, *op. cit.*, p. 105, n. 88.
28. *Ibid*, pp. 91-105.
29. Edward P. Echlin, S.J., "The Validity of Anglican Orders," *Journal of Ecumenical Studies,* vol. 7 (1970), pp. 266-281.
30. Cf. *Lutherans and Catholics in Dialogue: IV, Eucharist and Ministry* (Washington, 1970), pp. 7-23, *passim.*
31. Vatican II, *Unitatis Redintegratio*, nos. 19-23; Abbott, *op. cit.*, pp. 361-365.
32. Vatican II, *Lumen Gentium*, no. 8; Abbott, *op. cit.*, p. 23.
33. Mark 1:15.
34. Vatican II, *Lumen Gentium*, no. 3; Abbott, *op. cit.*, p. 16.
35. Hans Küng, *The Church* (New York, 1967), pp. 76ff.
36. Edward Schillebeeckx, O.P., "The Catholic Understanding of Office in the Church," *Theological Studies,* vol. 30 (1969), pp. 572-573.
37. *Ibid*.

PAPACY IN THE CHURCH OF THE FUTURE
(ROMAN CATHOLIC VIEW) — Henry G. J. Beck

1. However, E. E. Y. Hales: "The First Vatican Council," in G. J. Cuming and D. Baker (eds.): *Councils and Assem-*

REFERENCES

blies (Cambridge, 1971), pp. 329-44, and R. Aubert: *Vatican I* (Paris, 1964) make clear that the actual teaching of the 1869-70 synod is considerably more open than 20th century manualists realized.

2. See O. Cullman: *S. Pierre, disciple, apôtre, martyr* (Neuchatel, 1952); J. Lowe: *Saint Peter* (Oxford, 1956); O. Karrer: "Das Petrusamt in der Frühkirche," in E. Iserloh-P. Manns (eds.): *Festgabe Joseph Lortz* (Baden-Baden, 1958), I, pp. 507-25; M. M. Winter: *St. Peter and the Popes* (Baltimore, 1960); H. Küng: *The Church* (New York, 1967), pp. 444-80; B. Rigaux: "St. Peter in Contemporary Exegesis," in *Concilium* vol. 27 (1967), pp. 147-79; R. Pesch: "The Position and Significance of Peter in the Church of the NT," in *Concilium*, v. 64 (1971), pp. 21-35.

3. See Maximos IV: "Servant of the Servants of God," in H. Küng-Y. Congar-D. O'Hanlon (eds.): *Council Speeches of Vatican II* (Glen Rock, 1964), pp. 72-5; N. Afanasieff et al. (eds.): *Der Primat des Petrus in der orthodoxen Theologie* (Zurich, 1961); J. Meyendorff: *The Primacy of Peter in the Orthodox Church* (London, 1963); H. Küng (ed.): *Papal Ministry in the Church* (*Concilium*, v. 64, 1971).

4. See Cullman: *S. Pierre*, pp. 186-7; Lowe: *Saint Peter*, pp. 55-61; Trevor Jalland: *The Church and the Papacy* (London, 1944), pp. 55-56; Rigaux: "St. Peter," in *Concilium*, v. 27 (1967), pp. 171-4; E. Schweizer: *Church Order in the New Testament* (London, 1961), pp. 58-59.

5. Winter: *St. Peter and the Popes*, pp. 18-19 and O. Karrer: *Peter and the Church* (New York, 1963) take this position. Cullman: *S. Pierre*, pp. 187, 192ff., denies a succession to Peter's ministry.

6. A Roman succession to Peter and Paul is explicitly asserted by Irenaeus of Lyons: *Against the Heresies*, III, 3 (in Giles: *Documents Ilustrating Papal Authority, A.D. 95-454* (London, 1952), pp. 9-10). Our first evidence of the claim on the part of a Roman bishop occurs wth Stephen I (254-57), see Firmilian: *To Cyprian*, 17 (in Giles, p. 76).

7. See R. Pesch in *Concilium*, v. 64 (1971), pp. 31-35; Küng: *The Church*, pp. 476ff.

8. H. Denzinger-A. Schönmetzer: *Enchiridion Symbolorum* (ed. 32, 1963), nn. 3070, English transl. in J. F. Clarkson et al.: *The Church Teaches* (St. Louis, 1955), nn. 202, 216. Vatican II: *Lumen gentium*, nn. 18, 22, reaffirms Vatican I on the petrine primacy and employs Matthew 16 and John 21 (W. M. Abbott: *The Documents of Vatican II* (New York, 1966), pp. 38, 43).

9. Matthew 16 was cited in 422 by Pope Boniface I: "Manet beatum" (P. Jaffé-G. Wattenbach: *Regesta pontificum romanorum* (Leipzig, 1885), I, n. 365), also in 445 by Pope Leo I: "Divinae cultum" (ibid., I, n. 407). For Leo's teaching see T. Jalland: *The Life and Times of St. Leo the Great* (London, 1941), pp. 64-77.

10. The II Lyons declaration is in Denzinger-Schönmetzer, n. 861, and in *The Church Teaches*, n. 152; The Florentine decree is in DS, n. 1307, and CT, 164.

11. Cf. John 21, 7.

12. Cf. Acts 1, 22; 2, 36.

13. Cf. Vatican II: *Gaudium et spes*, nn. 44-5 (Abbott, pp. 245-8).

14. Matthew 7, 25. The Midrash Jalqut has the same view of a rock foundation; see Lowe: *St. Peter*, pp. 56-7.

15. F. V. Filson: "Peter," in *The Interpreter's Dictionary of the Bible* (New York, 1962), III, p. 752.

16. For the meaning of "key," cf. Isaiah 22, 22, and Revelation 3, 7.

17. See W. F. Arndt-F. W. Gingrich: *Greek-English Lexicon of the New Testament* (Chicago, 1957), p. 177, s. v. *deo*; also J. B. Bauer: "Binding and Loosing," in *Sacramentum Verbi* (New York, 1970), p. 67.

18. Matthew 18:18; cf. K. Rahner-J. Ratzinger: *The Episcopate and the Primacy* (New York, 1962), pp. 104-8.

19. Vatican I, DS, n. 3069: "explorata ecclesiae per orbem dispersae sententia"; Englished in CT, n. 216.

20. See M. Schmaus: "Pope," in K. Rahner et al. (eds.): *Sacramentum Mundi* (New York, 1970), V., p. 41; also Arndt-Gingrich, p. 775, s.v. *Sterizo*.

21. 1 Peter 5, 2-3; cf. B. Reicke: *The Epistles of James, Peter and Jude* (Anchor Bible, 37; New York, 1964), pp. 128-30.

22. There is a distinction between the two verbs for 'love';

agapao involves the will, *phileo* the emotions. Arndt-Gingrich, p. 4, suggests that in John 21, 15ff. they are used interchangeably.

23. The terms for 'lambs' and 'sheep' (*arnia, probata*) are distinguishable, but together they embrace the entire christian community; see Arndt-Gingrich, pp. 107, 710. Of the two verbs, *boskein* signifies 'feed,' *poimainein*, 'lead to pasture'; cf. Arndt - Gingrich, pp. 144, 690. *Poimen*, 'shepherd', whence the second verb is formed, is used by Christ of Himself in John 10:11.

24. The concept of God as shepherd and His people as sheep is found in Psalm 23, Ps. 88, 52, and especially in Ezechiel 34; in Ezechiel human shepherds of the people also are noted. In 2 Samuel 5:2, David is described as shepherd of God's people.

25. For a commentary on John 10, see R. E. Brown: *The Gospel according to John, I-XII* (Anchor Bible, 29; New York, 1966), pp. 383-400.

26. See M. Nicolau - I. Salaverri: *Sacrae theologiae summa* (ed. 4, Madrid, 1958), I, pp. 558-99; the articles of Ullmann and Sullivan in *New Catholic Encyclopedia*, X (1967), pp. 951-54, XI (1967), pp. 244-5, 779-80, and of Schmaus in *Sacramentum Mundi*, V (1970), pp. 40-50.

27. G. Schwaiger gives both summary and bibliography in *Sacramentum Mundi*, V (1970), pp. 50-60.

28. See the two studies of Maurice Bévenot: *St. Cyprian's De Unitate, Ch. 4, in the Light of the Manuscripts* (London, 1938), and St. Cyprian: *The Lapsed, The Unity of the Catholic Church* (Ancient Christian Writers, XXV; Westminster, Md., 1957).

29. In C. Mirbt: *Quellen zur Geschichte des Papsttums und des röm. Katholizismus* (5th ed., Tübingen, 1934), n. 372.

30. See W. Ullmann: *The Growth of Papal Government in the Middle Ages* (London, 1955) with the corrective of G. Barraclough: *The Medieval Papacy* (New York, 1968).

31. DS, n. 3064; Englished in CT, n. 211.

32. For the newer interpretations of this claim, see A. Ehrhardt: *The Apostolic Succession in the First Two Centuries of the Church* (London, 1953), H. Küng (ed.): *Apostolic Succession: Rethinking a Barrier to Unity* (*Concilium*, v. 34,

1968), W. Brenning in *Sacramentum Mundi,* I (1968), pp. 86-90, and R. E. Brown: *Priest and Bishop* (Paramus, 1970), pp. 47-86.

33. G. B. Wilson: "The Gift of Infallibility," *Theological Studies,* XXXI (1970), pp. 625-43; H. Küng: *Infallible? An Inquiry* (New York, 1971); E. Castelli (ed.): *L'infalli-bilité: Son aspect philosophique et théologique* (Paris, 1970); J. J. Kirvan (ed.): *The Infallibility Debate* (New York, 1971); J. J. Hughes, "Infallible? An Inquiry Considered," *Theological Studies,* XXXII (1971), pp. 183-207; J. T. Ford: "Infallibility — from Vatican I to the Present," *Journal of Ecumenical Studies,* VIII (1971), pp. 768-791; on the whole question, see Brian Tierney: *Origins of Papal Infallibility,* 1150-1350 (Leiden, Brill, 1972).

34. Papal infallibility, according to Vatican I, DS, n. 3074, is an exercise "ea infallibilitate . . . qua divinus Redemptor ecclesiam suam . . . instructam esse voluit"; concerning the employment of this papal authority, the same synod observes: "The Roman pontiffs . . . according as the condition of the times and the circumstances dictated, sometimes calling together ecumenical councils or sounding out the mind of the church throughout the whole world, sometimes through regional councils, or sometimes by using other helps which divine providence supplied, have, with the help of God, defined as to be held such matters as they had found consonant with the Holy Scriptures and with apostolic tradition" (CT, n. 216: original in DS, n. 3069). During the debate at the council (v.g., in J. D. Mansi: *Sacrorum concil-iorum collectio,* LII, 22c) it was recognized that the popes had a moral obligation to undertake a complete examination of questions to be defined: "eae omnes compleantur conditiones quæ requiruntur ut ab ipsorum definitionibus . . . omnis error excludatur." The affirmation (CT, n. 219: DS, n. 3074) that infallible papal decisions are "irreformable because of their nature, but not because of the agreement of the church" reflects Vatican I's preoccupation with a Gallican thesis (DS, n. 2284) on subsequent church approval of papal teaching. It does not reject the need for the pope's consulting the church before his definition; see H. Fries: "Ex sese, non ex consensu ecclesiæ," in *Volk Gottes: Fest-*

schrift J. Hofer (1967), pp. 480-500, and his summary in *Sacramentum Mundi*, III (1969), p. 135.

35. H. Häring: "Can a Petrine Office be Meaningful in the Church?", *Concilium*, v. 64 (1971), p. 145.

36. I find heartening the following NC news dispatch of Pope Paul's general audience of August 25, 1971 at Castel Gandolfo:

Authority in the Church must be exercised as a "service" to its members, Pope Paul VI told his weekly general audience August 25.

He stressed that the "genuine concept of authority in the church" must not be thought of in terms of "despotism, pride, selfishness or triumphalism." . . . He admitted that, historically, temporal and spiritual authority has at times been treated as personal power "not only in Rome but in many other local European churches."

He described a genuine concept of church authority modeled on Christ who was at the service of God the Father in carrying out the divine will, this way: "The exercise of authority in the church is called ministry. . . . The authority of the church is of pastoral nature. . . . It must be in pursuit of the common good and a service, neither light nor easy, for the benefit of those who are in need of it. Its style must be evangelical, that is, pastoral, and its forms appropriate and legitimate so that it may show itself as the manifestation of the virtues of Christ."

—*St. Louis Review,* Sept. 3, 1971, p. 2.

PAPACY IN THE CHURCH OF THE FUTURE
(ANGLICAN PERSPECTIVE) — J. Robert Wright

1. A. G. Dickens and Dorothy Carr, *The Reformation in England to the Accession of Elizabeth I* (London 1967), 46-89; A. G. Dickens, *The English Reformation* (London 1964), 113-122.

2. See for example, J. J. Scarisbrick, "Clerical Taxation in England 1485-1547," *Journal of Ecclesiastical History* XI (1960), 41-54; W. E. Lunt, *Financial Relations of the Papacy with England 1327-1534* (Cambridge, Mass., 1962),

ch. viii; E. J. Bicknell, *A Theological Introduction to the Thirty-Nine Articles of the Church of England*, rev. H. J. Carpenter (London 1955), 426-9.

3. See, e.g., J. W. Gray, "Canon Law in England—Some Reflections on the Stubbs-Maitland Controversy," *Studies in Church History* III, ed. G. J. Cuming (London 1966), 48-68; D. Hay, "The Church of England in the Later Middle Ages," *History* LIII:177 (February 1968), 35-50; and *The English Church and The Papacy in the Middle Ages*, ed. C. H. Lawrence (London 1965).

4. T. M. Powicke, *The Reformation in England* (London 1941), ch. 1; Dickins, op. cit., p. 107 and n. 22; P. M. Dawley, *John Whitgift and the English Reformation* (N. Y. 1954), 1-24.

5. See, for example, the assertions in the Bishops' Book of 1537; P. Hughes, *The Reformation in England* (London 1963), II, 30-35.

6. Supra, n. 3.

7. Cf. G. J. Cuming, *A History of Anglican Liturgy* (London 1969), 54.

8. *The First and Second Prayer Books of Edward VI*, introd. by E. C. S. Gibson (Everyman's Library, London 1910), 232, 362. This clause was, however, omitted from the Litany during the reign of Mary Tudor; W. P. Haugaard, "The English Litany from Henry to Elizabeth," *Anglican Theological Review* LI:3 (July 1969), 179, 188-9.

9. Ed. J. E. Booty (Ithaca 1963), 91-3, cf. 25-6. See also H. R. McAdoo, *The Spirit of Anglicanism: A Survey of Anglican Theological Method in the Seventeenth Century* (N. Y. 1965), chs. ix and x, for discussion of this approach. For some other particular examples, see the passages from William Laud, Isaac Barrow, and John Bramhall quoted in *Anglicanism*, ed. P. E. More and F. L. Cross (London 1935), 53-72.

10. Hughes, op. cit., III, 166-7, and cf. p. 77; More and Cross, op. cit., 69-71 (James Ussher).

11. For a start see G. H. Tavard, *The Quest for Catholicity* (N. Y. 1964).

12. The learned Hooker is, by contrast with Jewel on this

point, considerably more judicious. *Ecclesiastical Polity* (1594), bk. iv.

13. *The Works of W. Chillingworth, M.A.* . . . twelfth ed., London 1836, 683ff.

14. *The Whole Works of the Right Rev. Jeremy Taylor* . . . , (ed.) Reginald Heber. Third ed. of the collected works, London, 1839; e.g., vol. x, 177ff., 297, 331ff., vol. xi, 665-7.

15. More and Cross, op. cit., 72.

16. Ibid., 68.

17. These and the following three views are quoted from J. C. Dickinson, "Papal Authority — the Background," in *Infallibility in the Church,* ed. M. D. Goulder (London 1968), 50-1.

18. London 1936, 227-8.

19. London 1957, 125-6.

20. *Church Times* (London), 8 July 1966, 10 February 1967. Italicized words in parentheses supplied.

21. *Holy Cross Magazine,* (West Park, N.Y.), July 1967, 2-5; cf. *American Church News* (Pelham Manor, N.Y.), 27 September 1967, and *The Little Chronicle* (Mt. Sinai, L.I., N.Y.), LII:2, November 1970.

22. *Pilgrim from Canterbury Visits Friars at Graymoor* (Garrison, N.Y., 1972), 19. For similar statements cf. the *Church Times* (London), 29 November 1967: "I don't think that Christendom as a whole would accept the Pope as infallible in defining faith and morals. But I do think Christendom as a whole might accept the Pope as presiding bishop among the bishops of the world"; also in J. B. Simpson, *The Hundredth Archbishop of Canterbury* (N. Y. 1962), 162: ". . . I would be willing to accept the Pope as a presiding bishop, but not as infallible. I would be willing to call him *primus inter pares,* first among equals."

23. *The Lambeth Conference 1968: Resolutions and Reports* (London 1968), 137-8.

24. *Herder Correspondence* VI:1 (January 1969), 27; J. B. Simpson and E. M. Story, *The Long Shadows of Lambeth X* (N. Y. 1969), 229-233. The 1968 Conference met from July 25-August 25. It is interesting to compare the effect of the 1870 infallibility decree upon the statement of the sec-

ond Lambeth Conference of 1878: "The fact that a solemn protest is raised in so many Churches and Christian communities throughout the world against the usurpations of the See of Rome, and against the novel doctrines promulgated by its authority, is a subject for thankfulness to Almighty God. All sympathy is due from the Anglican Church to the Churches and individuals protesting against these errors, and labouring, it may be, under special difficulties from the assaults of unbelief as well as from the pretensions of Rome. . . . It is therefore our duty to warn the faithful that the act done by the Bishop of Rome, in the Vatican Council, in the year 1870 — whereby he asserted a supremacy over all men in matters both of faith and morals, on the ground of an assumed infallibility — was an invasion of the attributes of the Lord Jesus Christ." Quoted from W. H. Van de Pol, *Anglicanism in Ecumenical Perspective* (Pittsburgh 1965), 42.

25. E.g., Dickinson, op. cit., 53-8; T. M. Parker, quoted in H. Burn-Murdoch, *The Development of the Papacy* (London, 1954), 8.

26. E.g., the "Utrecht Declaration" of 1889, and the conference of Old Catholic bishops and theologians in 1967, summarized in H. Küng, *Infallible? An Inquiry* (Garden City, N.Y. 1971), 132-4.

27. J. Meyendorff. *Orthodoxy and Catholicity* (N. Y. 1966), ch. 3 and esp. pp. 73-6; A. Schmemann, "The Idea of Primacy in Orthodox Ecclesiology," *Saint Vladimir's Seminary Quarterly*, vol. 4 (N.Y., 1960), p. 49.

28. See D. W. Allen and A. M. Allchin, "Primacy and Collegiality: An Anglican View," *Journal of Ecumenical Studies* II (Winter 1965), 63-80.

29. For a "traditional" Anglican refutation of the 1870 definition, see Burn-Murdoch, op. cit., 397-410.

30. The best summaries of the current state of this debate may, in my opinion, be found in F. Oakley, *Council over Pope?* (N. Y. 1969); Oakley, "The 'New Conciliarism' and Its Implications: A Problem in History and Hermeneutics," in *Journal of Ecumenical Studies* VIII:4 (Fall 1971), 815-40; B. Tierney's review of Oakley's book (op. cit., in *The Jurist* (1970:3), 398-9; R. E. McNally, "Conciliarism and

the Papacy," in Catholic Theological Society of America, *Proceedings,* vol. 25 (1970), N.Y. 1971, pp. 13-30; and P. de Vooght, "The Results of Recent Historical Research on Conciliarism," in *Concilium,* vol. 64 (*Papal Ministry in the Church,* ed. H. Küng), N.Y. 1971, 148-157.

31. Qualifications would have to be made in specific cases, but generally this list can include Oakley, Küng, Tierney, and McNally. They would be opposed, in varying degrees, by Gill, Jedin, Franzen, de Vooght, and Tavard. (For the last of these see his *The Church Tomorrow* (N. Y. 1965), p. 40, n. 1. For the others, see supra n. 30.)

32. Leiden 1972.

33. See review by R. E. McNally in *Journal of Ecumenical Studies* IX:1 (Winter 1972), 130-2.

34. For a statement of this approach see J. T. Ford, "Infallibility — From Vatican I to the Present," in *Journal of Ecumenical Studies* VIII:4 (Fall 1971), 769, and also Tierney, in ibid., 844.

35. See especially H. J. McSorley, "A Response to Küng's Inquiry on Infallibility," in *Worship* 45:6 (June-July 1971), 314-25, and 45:7 (August-September 1971), 384-404. Also K. Rahner, "A Critique of Hans Küng," in *Homiletic and Pastoral Review,* May 1971, 10-26.

36. Cf. A. M. Farrer, "Infallibility and Historical Revelation" in Goulder, op. cit., 23.

37. N. Y. 1967, 478.

38. *National Catholic Reporter* 7:21 (March 26, 1971), p. 12-A.

39. *America,* 24 April 1971, p. 428.

40. "Contemporary Understanding of the Irreformability of Dogma," in Catholic Theological Society of America, op. cit., 134-5.

41. *The Tablet,* 3 April 1971, p. 329; cf. pp. 328-30, 372-5, 398-400, 433-5.

42. Review by C. Hay of *L'Infallibilité pontificale* in *One in Christ* VII:2-3 (1971), 301-2.

43. Quoted in Ford, op. cit., 785.

44. "Theses on Future Forms of the Ministry," *Journal of Ecumenical Studies* V (1968), 728.

45. *Theological Studies,* vol. 31 (1970), 640, 642.

46. "*The* Ecumenical Problem Today — Papal Infallibility,"

Journal of Ecumenical Studies VIII:4 (Fall 1971), 751-67; quote from p. 762.

47. Burn-Murdoch, op. cit., 409.
48. For this terminology, see Emmanuel Lanne, "Pluralism and Unity — The Possibility of a Variety of Typologies within the Same Ecclesial Allegiance," in *One in Christ* VI:3 (1970), 430-51, and esp. p. 447; and Jan Cardinal Willebrands, "A variety of 'typoi' within the communion of the Church," ibid. VII:1 (1971), 118-121.
49. See point 4(a) in "Doctrinal Agreement and Christian Unity: Methodological Considerations," the agreed joint statement of ARC XI (Anglican-Roman Catholic Consultation), 23 January 1972, published in *Ecumenical Trends* 1:2 (May 1972), p. 7. "Within a single Church one and the same formula often receives different theological interpretations."
50. *The Documents of Vatican II*, ed. W. M. Abbott (N. Y. 1966), 37-56 (Dogmatic Constitution on the Church, ch. iii).
51. The principle here implied is suggested in point 4(b) of the ARC XI statement (see note 49, supra): "Because the same mystery can sometimes be conveyed more effectively by different formulas in different cultural contexts, one may support a variety of theological expressions among different groups of Christians."
52. See B. C. Butler, "United Not Absorbed," a suggestion on the possibility of corporate reunion that appeared in *The Tablet*, 7 March 1970, 220-1.

REGIONAL UNION
A THEOLOGICAL APPROACH — William F. Murphy

1. R. Bellarminus, *Opera Omnia*, v. II. Napoli, 1864.
2. Ibid., v. III, c. 1. Napoli, 1864.
3. I am indebted to E. Lanne, O.S.B., for his clear exposition of this point in his article "Local Church, its Catholicity and Apostolicity" in *One in Christ* 7, (1971), 288-313.
4. Ignatius Antioch. *ad Phil.* and passim in his *Letters*.
5. *Hist. Eccl.* X, 4.
6. Cf. article "Evêque" in *Catholicisme* IV, 781-94.

REFERENCES

7. Cf. J. W. O'Malley, "Reform, Historical Consciousness and Vatican II's aggiornamento," *Theological Studies* 32 (1971), 573-601.
8. Cf. J. Colson, "Qu'est-ce qu'un diocèse?", *Nouvelle Revue Théologique* 75 (1953), 471-97; Y. Congar, *The Mystery of the Church*, Baltimore 1960; J. Ratzinger, "Primat, episcopat und Successio Apostolica," *Catholica* 13 (1959), 260-77; and J. A. Möhler, *Die Einheit in der kirche*, Tübingen (1825).
9. W. M. Abbott, ed., *The Documents of Vatican II*, N.Y. 1966, 152; cf. Section 42.
10. Abbott, 32.
11. Abbott, 44, 50, 51-2.
12. *Christus Dominus*, Chapter 2, Section II; Abbott, 403.
13. *Acta Apostolicae Sedis* 59 (25 May 1967), 539-73, esp. 545.
14. Cf. address of Paul VI to the Italian Week of Pastoral Aggiornamento, 9 September 1971, as reported in *La Documentation Catholique* 68, 856-58.
15. Cf. Cyprian, *Letters*, 66, 83 and 33. Cf. B. Batazolle, "L'évêque et la vie chrétienne au sein de l'église locale," in Y. Congar and B. DuPuy, *L'Episcopat et l'Eglise Universelle*, Paris 1964.
16. E.g., K. McNamara, "The Theological Position of the Bishop," *Furrow* 22 (1971), 476-96.
17. Cf. R. Schnackenburg, "Apostolicity: Present Position of the Studies," *One in Christ* 6 (1970), 243-73.
18. Cf. Mark 6:7-13; Luke 10; Matthew 28:18-20; Luke 24:47.
19. M. J. LeGuillou, *Mission et Unité*, Paris 1968, 139; transl. by the author. Cf. also his "Mission as an Ecclesiological Theme," *Concilium* 13, 81-130; "Mission in the Spirit of Ecumenism," *One in Christ* 3 (1967), 11-34.
20. "Mission in the Spirit of Ecumenism," *One in Christ* 3 (1967), 13ff.

A SOCIOLOGIST LOOKS AT ECUMENISM

Eugene J. Schallert, S.J.

1. *Acta Apostolicae Sedis* 57, p. 114.
2. *Unitatis Redintegratio*, 13. Cf. W. M. Abbott, ed., *The Doc-*

uments of Vatican II, Guild Press, New York, 1966, p. 356.
3. Augustin Cardinal Bea, *Unity of Christians,* Herder and Herder, New York, 1962, p. 73.
4. *Gaudium et Spes,* 62. Cf. Abbott, *op. cit.,* 269.
5. Cf. *ibid.,* 200-03. *Gaudium et Spes,* 3 and 4.

UNIFYING ROMAN CATHOLIC AND EPISCOPAL

PARISHES – George A. Shipman

A NOTE ON BACKGROUND READING

Specific sources for the ideas and points of view set forth in this paper are not readily designated. But two streams of influence in the professional literature are primary. One is the field of the sociology of religion with special reference to the United States. The other is organization theory and its projections to organization analysis. The idea of the Christian community is of course a specialized one, not to be equated with the other more generalized uses of the concept. It is probably closer to the idea of a special social system, which over time acquires particularized attributes distinguishing it from other social collectivities with which it interacts. The reference in the text to Glock and Stark is to Charles Y. Glock and Rodney Stark, *Religion and Society in Tension* (Rand McNally, Chicago, 1965).

In the field of the sociology of religion, apart from the familiar textbooks, the chapter by Charles Y. Glock, "The Sociology of Religion," in Merton, Broom and Cottrell (editors), *Sociology Today, Problems and Prospects* (Basic Books, New York, 1959), Chapter 9, is an excellent overview as of that time. Most valuable, to this reader at least, are Talcott Parsons, *Structure and Process in Modern Societies* (Free Press of Glencoe, Illinois, 1960) particularly Chapter 10, "Some Comments on the Pattern of Religious Organization in the United States," and the contributions by Parsons, "Christianity and Modern Industrial Society," and by Thomas F. O'Dea, "Sociological Dilemmas: Five Paradoxes of Institutionalization" in Edward A. Tiryakian (editor), *Sociological Theory, Values and Cultural Change* (Free Press of Glencoe, Illinois, 1963). In addition, the *International Encyclopedia of the Social Sciences* (Macmillan Company and Free Press, 1968) contains several very useful articles, particularly Parsons, "Christianity," and Bryan Wilson, "Religious Organizations."

The literature in the field of organization theory and analysis is another matter. The treatment of religious organizations, and particularly the parish or congregation as a voluntary affiliation, is scanty by comparison to that of business, industrial and governmental organizations. The ideas used in the text have been strongly influenced by the writings of Talcott Parsons, but the particularized approaches and points of view should not be ascribed to him. For these the writer assumes full responsibility. The reader who wants a knowledgeable and rather compact treatment of thinking about organizations should use James D. Thompson, *Organizations in Action* (McGraw Hill, New York, 1967). A very useful overview of approaches to organizational development is in Daniel Katz and Robert L. Kahn, *The Social Psychology of Organizations* (Wiley, New York, 1966), Chapter 13, "Organizational Change." The volume by Warren G. Bennis, *Changing Organizations* (McGraw Hill, New York, 1966), is also most valuable.

EPISCOPALIANS AND ROMAN CATHOLICS

PARTICIPANTS

Edwin G. Bennett. Baltimore, Maryland
Van S. Bowen. New York, New York
W. Nelson Bump. New York, New York
Michael Cantley. Brooklyn, New York
Thomas P. Coffey. Denville, New Jersey
John C. Cosby. Springfield, Massachusetts
Titus Cranny. Providence, Rhode Island
Peter Day. New York, New York
Edmund Delaney. Garrison, New York
Robert M. Dresser. Stamford, Connecticut
John T. Ford. Washington, D.C.
James J. Gardiner. Akron, Ohio
Arthur Gouthro. South Bend, Indiana
John F. Hamblin. St. Petersburg, Florida
Phebe Hoff. Richmond, Virginia
Jacqueline Kelley. San Francisco, California
Jeremiah Kelliher. Garrison, New York
Edward Kilmartin. Cambridge, Massachusetts
Timothy MacDonald. Garrison, New York
Gary MacEoin. Nutley, New Jersey
Henry Marchese. Cumberland, Rhode Island
Josephine Marie. Brooklyn, New York
Edna McCallion. Pelham, New York
Daniel McKenzie. Washington, D.C.
Edward J. McLean. Hartford, Connecticut
Philip J. Murnion. New York, New York
Shunji F. Nishi. Berkeley, California
Richard W. Rousseau. New York, New York
Joseph Scerbo. Berkeley, California
W. Taylor Stevenson. Milwaukee, Wisconsin
Ralph Thomas. Garrison, New York
John F. Wessel. Cleveland, Ohio
J. Stuart Wetmore. New York, New York
Polly Wiley, Pound Ridge, New York

REFERENCES

SPONSORS

THE GRAYMOOR ECUMENICAL INSTITUTE is a department of the Franciscan Friars of the Atonement which initiates, studies, and promotes ecumenical activities both inside and outside the community of Atonement Friars.

The Ecumenical Institute assists in developing policy with regard to the ecumenical apostolate of the Society of the Atonement and also serves other churches and Christians as a clearing house of ecumenical news and information. It promotes and sponsors theological meetings, retreats, lectures, prayer movements and dialogues.

THE EPISCOPAL CHURCH FOUNDATION is an independent corporation of laymen and laywomen established in 1949 by Bishop Henry Knox Sherrill to provide financial and direct action capabilities to the Episcopal Church. It is governed by a Board of Directors made up of some 50 nationally known business and professional men and women, and administered by a small staff in New York and Chicago.

The Foundation's basic activities break down into three areas: the Graduate Fellowship Program, the Revolving Loan Fund, and Projects and Research.